Follow Your Dreams
Dixie Madsen

D1559631

Life is an Ultramarathon
Embrace the Journey

THE DIXIE MADSEN STORY

Life is an Ultramarathon

Embrace the Journey

THE DIXIE MADSEN STORY

Dixie Madsen

WITH SID SHAPIRA

www.mascotbooks.com

Life is an Ultramarathon:
Embrace the Journey
The Dixie Madsen Story

For more information, please contact:
Mascot Books
620 Herndon Parkway #320
Herndon, VA 20170
info@mascotbooks.com

Library of Congress Control Number: 2018905668

CPSIA Code: PROPM0918A
ISBN-13: 978-1-64307-091-9

Printed in the United States

This book is dedicated to my wonderful children, grandchildren, and great-grandchildren. I hope my story inspires you to follow your dreams – anything is possible!

"Falling down is a part of life; getting back up is living."

–Dixie

Table of Contents

Foreword

Dixie Madsen is one of the most extraordinary women I have had the good fortune to call a friend, mentor, and absolute inspiration.

I met Dixie many years ago at an ultramarathon competition. When I met Dixie, the first thing I noticed was the beauty and kindness in her eyes. I always look into someone's eyes when I first meet them because I learn so much. The moment I met her, I knew she was a woman of deep faith who truly embraced life in each moment. I felt an intimate connection with Dixie as a soul sister!

The ninth of 16 children in her family, Dixie was raised in a foster home. I can't imagine the childhood Dixie had, but I can tell you that Dixie never let anything stand in her way of giving life her absolute best, beautiful, and perfect effort.

Dixie is a true warrior who stands tall in the face of adversity. She is a woman of amazing dignity, grace, and faith.

Every single person reading this book will be touched in many ways by the attitude of gratitude that Dixie has shown and given to her life.

From bodybuilding to running the hardest foot race on earth – the Badwater 135 – through extreme heat and conditions, Dixie will inspire you to believe that anything is possible if you have the desire and conviction. Dixie will get you off the sofa and help guide you to realizing that your own journey here on earth matters. Dixie is a treasure and a gift to us all.

–Lisa Smith-Batchen
Jackson, Wyoming

Lisa Smith-Batchen is a coach, motivational speaker, and athlete, who is a 10-time participant in the Badwater 135 and the only woman to have completed the Badwater Quad (594 miles).

CHAPTER 1

Up for the
challenge

A 63-year-old woman isn't supposed to be doing this sort of thing. Perhaps something more sedentary – like solving the Sunday crossword puzzle or reading a romance novel – might be more appropriate. But not this type of challenge. Then, again, I've never been one to back down from anything.

Here I was about to tackle the most demanding and extreme running competition anywhere on the planet. And I couldn't have been more excited! The oldest woman competing in this race, there was no doubt in my mind I was going to finish it!

The Badwater 135, a rugged competition covering 135 miles nonstop from Death Valley to Mount Whitney, California, is regarded as the world's most challenging running event. People from all over the world gather to participate in this grueling race.

I was confident heading into the race. I had already broken 15 American records at that time for women in the 50-60 years age division. There were a number of races leading up to this mid-summer event and runners must achieve a qualifying time to enter Badwater. My times were excellent and I comfortably qualified.

I arrived at Badwater a day before the race. I was well trained. My mind was set to have a strong race with the support of my loving husband, a good crew, and plenty of faith in my abilities. I left the rest in God's hands.

The starting line is at Badwater Basin, Death Valley, which marks the lowest elevation in North America at 282 feet below sea level. The race finishes at Whitney Portal at 8,374 feet which is the trailhead to the Mount Whitney summit, the highest point in the contiguous United States. The Badwater 135 covers three mountain ranges for a total of 14,600 feet of cumulative vertical ascent and 6,100 feet of cumulative descent. During the race, competitors travel to places or landmarks with names like Mushroom Rock, Furnace Creek, Salt Creek, Devil's Cornfields, Devil's Golf Course, Stovepipe Wells, Pandemic Springs, Keeler, Alabama Hills, and Lone Pine.

The emotions running through my head at the start of the race were of pure excitement and anticipation. I never had any doubt I would finish the race. After all, I had been running 100-mile races – ultramarathons, as they are called – for some time now. I knew that once I started something, I was going to finish it. I just knew.

Apart from some friction between two members of my crew

Start of the Badwater 135 at 5:00 a.m. Dixie behind the 't' in Badwater

who had begun to argue with each other, everything seemed to be under control at the starting line. I was in the 5:00 a.m. start group in a place they call the lowest part in the hemisphere. By midday, the temperature was expected to reach 128 degrees.

The preparation for this race was unbelievable. It cost more than $2,000 just for supplies. You needed two vehicles, a group of runners to accompany you, and people to provide nourishment and supplies. Our supply wagon needed to accommodate our crew of five.

Every mile, my crew would meet me and hand me two bottles, one filled with nutrition and the other with solid ice and just a bit of water. By the end of the mile, the bottle of ice would be completely melted. I would put ice on my head, my hat, and on my handkerchief which was wrapped around my neck.

I took one small break early on the second day. My husband, Kendall, told me I needed to lay down for a few minutes. I was used to taking 15-minute breaks when I was working as a nurse, so I was able to power nap for 15 minutes. He placed a bed down for me in the shade. I laid down for 15 minutes and then my internal alarm clock sounded.

"You're not getting up now," said Kendall.

"No, I'm fine," I said.

"Lay down for 10 more minutes," ordered Kendall.

During the first day of the competition, I stopped at one of the eight aid stations along the route. A camera crew had been following the runners to allow people to monitor the race on the Internet. I laid down for just a few seconds at the aid station and, wouldn't you know it, the camera crew captured this moment. And that's the image my daughter, Debbie, saw on her computer in Virginia. She was scared to death.

I ran all day and night. Around midnight on the first day, I lost everything. I threw up all over the place. I told Kendall to bring me the supply bag that was labeled "cleanup." The bag had fresh shirts, shorts, socks, and everything. In the dark, I cleaned myself up, poured water all over me, and pronounced myself ready to go again.

In running gear with plenty of sun protection at Badwater 135

As I started down the road, I began to see lounge chairs off to one side. Then, I started to see recliners on the other side. I was hallucinating. My mind wanted to go to sleep.

I had completed many 100-mile races over the years, but I had never hallucinated before. However, this notion was not unfamiliar to me. The year before, I witnessed a similar episode as part of the crew for a runner named Jim.

"See those people having a picnic over there," said Jim. "I want some of their watermelon."

"Jim, there's nobody picnicking over there," I said. "It's pitch dark."

Now, it was me experiencing this phenomenon.

The next night as I was running on the road from Lone Pine to Whitney Portal, I developed a huge blister on my right foot. One of my crew members, Sandy, was with me. She was one of the five runners that ran alongside me to keep me company.

As soon as we got on the road to Lone Pine, I witnessed the most beautiful design I had ever seen in my life. I began to see mice, elephants, and rabbits in all these different colors, interwoven with pink and white candy canes.

I thought to myself, *Wow, if I were an artist, I would go home, patent this pattern, and paint this design in children's bedrooms.*

As Sandy and I were going up the road, we made a left-hand turn. I had been to Lone Pine several times before and had run in that area. I didn't remember there being a turn to the left.

But Sandy turned that way and I followed. And the crew followed along. All of a sudden, as we went up the road a little further, I saw a campground.

"We must have taken a wrong turn," I said to Sandy.

When we made that turn, my hallucinations disappeared. I didn't see those animals or that pattern anymore.

Sandy said she would run down the road to determine if we had indeed made a wrong turn. As she proceeded down the road for a bit, I started down the road as well. Sure enough, we had made a wrong turn. At this point I was really pushing to make the cut-off time of 48 hours.

Magically, as soon as we got back on the proper road, the animals and that wonderful, colored pattern came back into view.

We began our climb up to Mount Whitney Portal. By that time, my foot was hurting so much I had to remove my right shoe.

I ran the rest of the way with one shoe on and one shoe off. It certainly relieved the pressure. I also discovered that I had the best running socks in the world. When I finished the race, there wasn't even a hole in the exposed sock.

Meanwhile, my crew had all fallen asleep up the road, except for Kendall. He knew that I should be arriving about then, so he came back running down the road to see where I was. He noticed Sandy and me with flashlights headed in his direction.

Kendall started to hallucinate himself. He began to see flying saucers. Of course, everyone had stayed awake as long as I had. I had booked hotel rooms for my crew to get some rest, but none of them wanted to sleep in the rooms. They wanted to stay right there with me.

In spite of the wrong turn, I still managed to complete the race in 47 hours and four minutes, nearly an hour ahead of the cut-off time.

A race of this magnitude never goes off without a hiccup or two. But, I knew somehow, some way, I was going to finish it. It was just a matter of how I got there.

It was traumatic in that there was some conflict at the start of the race. I had written a book of instructions before the race as I did before each ultramarathon. I like to plan every step of the race. This book was placed on the dashboard of each car. And Kendall was going to video me. Well, none of the crew looked at my instructions before and during the race. And, the crew couldn't stand each other as well. Not a good combination.

I made the mistake of having all but one ultrarunner on my crew. They had upcoming races and were more interested in logging their own miles by running with me rather than following the instructions I had specified. Meanwhile, Kendall was desperately trying to get everyone to do what they were supposed to do and video me at the same time. The video turned out horribly.

With crew at Badwater 135 in 2000

Two weeks after the race, I was contacted by a television program, *To Tell the Truth*. They wanted to know if I had a video from the race since they wanted to feature me on their program. After looking at my video, they declined. There was a set of twins who had run the race the year before. They had a video that was done professionally and they ended up being featured on the program.

I was unique in that I was the oldest female competitor in the event. And, I'm proud to say that I still hold the record for being the oldest woman (63 years old) to have completed the race in a sub 48-hour time (47 hours, 4 minutes). Not only that, I finished fifth overall among women and twentieth overall in the entire field!

The idea that you can accomplish anything you put your mind to was reinforced during these two eventful and exhausting days in the summer of 2000.

This race was emotionally and physically draining. Certainly, it was a big accomplishment for me, but it's something I would never want to put my body through again.

In my mind, I had made the decision I would complete it and my body came along for the ride. And what a ride it was!

CHAPTER 2
Chaotic childhood

I was born on February 26, 1937 at 11:40 a.m. in St. George, Utah. Clearly, I must have been a major letdown to my parents. They were hoping for a boy. They had even picked out a name – Andy.

So, when their baby girl arrived, my parents had to scramble to come up with a name. As St. George was the home of Dixie Junior College (now Dixie State University) and the name "Dixie" was painted in white on the mountain over-

Dixie at 10 months old –
Dec. 1937

Dixie etched on the hill in St. George

looking the town, it seemed a natural fit. So, my mother, Alta, proudly announced her little girl would be called Dixie. And, the name stuck.

Dixie fits me and has all of my life. A cute name, it also implies a certain spirit and spunkiness. In that respect, they couldn't have chosen a better name.

To say my childhood was unsettled would be a blatant understatement. The terms "tumultuous," "chaotic," and "bizarre" come to mind. My formative years were definitely anything but stable and idyllic.

In order, I was the ninth of 16 children born to my parents. Only eight survived childbirth.

Map of St. George, Utah

Tragically, my parents lost three sets of twin boys, and two baby boys in the first several hours of their lives. I learned this many years later while doing genealogical research on our family tree.

The babies had turned blue and died. The medical term "blue baby" means a baby with a blue complexion from lack of oxygen in the blood due to a congenital defect of the heart or major blood vessels.

I'll never forget the day my dad brought home my little brother in a suitcase to show him to us kids before he took him to Richfield to be buried. I was in the first grade at the time.

My baby brother had died within two days of birth with the Rh factor in his blood. His death was caused by my mother's and father's blood types not matching. It was so heartbreaking.

Unfortunately, sadness and disappointment would be a constant throughout my childhood.

My father, Marion, drank a lot and the consequences weren't pretty.

Often, my father would return home drunk after being on the road as a miscellaneous hide and junk salesman. There always seemed to be a bottle of Four Roses whiskey in the jockey

Parents at their 50th wedding anniversary in 1972 in Salt Lake City

box (glove compartment) of his truck. When my father came home in that condition, most of the time we would make ourselves scarce. We would hide or just get out of the way. He and my mother would immediately start to fight over something I can't even remember now. And, he would beat her very badly.

One time, I tried to break up the fight by pulling on his bib overalls while screaming, "Daddy, please stop beating momma!"

I guess I thought I could stop him. It didn't work and the fighting persisted.

Not that my mother was an angel. In fact, she was anything but. Maybe after 16 pregnancies, she didn't quite feel the love for her children.

She seemed to think I was always in need of a beating. As a result, I became quite familiar with her belt. While she beat all us kids, for some reason I was the most frequent target.

When my father started producing rodeo events, my mother began wearing pants quite regularly. She became rather attached to a belt that had blue, red, and green glass stones on it. While she favored that belt, I wasn't so fond of it. Oh, how it hurt! It left welts on my skin for days. It seemed she couldn't stop with just one or two lashes. She kept on walloping.

Those beatings only confirmed in my mind that she was one mean woman. Thinking back, I don't ever recall my mother telling me she loved me or embracing me with a warm hug. Not exactly a loving and nurturing soul.

As I've grown up and had time to reflect on my mother's life, maybe her being pregnant every year or so didn't leave much time to spread the love around to anyone.

One year, I wanted to do something special for my mother's birthday. I went without lunch at school for a while and bought my mother a present with the money I saved. I can't remember what I purchased. But, I do know that when I gave her the gift and explained to her how I saved for it, she immediately loosened her belt and gave me a whipping for going without my lunch. As the old saying goes, "no good deed goes unpunished."

My father was one of three children. He had a brother, Arvil, a restaurant owner in Beaver, Utah, and a sister, Viola, who lived in Oakland, California. They weren't close at all.

Even though my father was an alcoholic, he was kind and gentle to me. We enjoyed some special moments together. On school breaks and during the summertime, he would often ask me to accompany him on road trips.

He would travel to suppliers to purchase pelts, deer hides, batteries, and that sort of thing. We would hop into his big truck and head down Highway 91 and back up Highway 89. My little brother, Pete, was too young to travel, so it was just me and my dad. I was in grade school and I always carried a big coloring book with me. We'd stop at restaurants and stay at motels along the way. And he would buy me treats. I really loved these excursions with my father. This father-daughter time was very important to me.

My mother was the only girl of 10 children. As a result, she was pampered as a child. My mother, who was very pretty, was always conscious of her appearance. She never did her own hair and went to the beauty shop every week to have her hair done. I marveled at her beauty considering she had given birth to 16 children!

The one thing she enjoyed doing with her daughters was taking us to the beauty shop just before the start of the school year and arranging for us to get a perm. Essentially, we had our hair fried at the beauty shop with electric wires clamped onto our hair. When they turned the machines off, our hair was frizzled. It was no wonder my hair never looked great.

We didn't have a bathroom inside the house. We had an outhouse until I was about 11 years old. So, every morning, like clockwork, my mother would set up in front of the kitchen sink to wash her face and put on her makeup.

My mother never seemed to show the same devotion and commitment to her children as she did to her appearance. She was not a loving person.

As I became an adult, I began to realize the constant beatings she inflicted on me were her way of relieving all the anxiety she was feeling. As a child, I didn't understand this. But I put it together later, and reckoned she had to have some way of releasing the turmoil going on inside her.

The house that I grew up in was situated on a 20-acre farm off Highway 91 between Springville and Spanish Fork, Utah. Neighbors were quite a distance apart so we never had any friends to play with nearby.

Family farm in Springville –
Dixie returned there in 2010

Our house had four bedrooms with a large living room and a large kitchen.

My mother cooked on a coal stove with a tank on the far end which we kept filled with water for washing up and taking baths.

Saturday nights were reserved for bath nights. It's hard for people today to imagine that back then there weren't many indoor bathrooms so we didn't bathe except to get ready for church on Sunday. Then, the number three wash tub was brought out. Hot water was transferred from the water tank on the stove to the tub sitting in the middle of the kitchen floor.

We started with the oldest child – who got the warmest and cleanest water – and worked our way down to the youngest. Thinking back, I'm not sure the youngest got any cleaner than he or she was before the bath.

Of course, as the next child entered the number three tub, a pitcher full of hot water would be added. The soap we used would be the bar soap that my mother had made from the grease saved from cooking and whatever else she added to make our soap back then. This bar soap was also used for washing our hair, along with water from the drain barrel – rain water caught in a big barrel.

I never knew what it was like to sleep in a bed alone until after my older siblings were married and gone. Then, it was just me, Pete, and my little niece – who we were raising most of the time – all in the same bed. Then, when I began to run away from home, I was placed in a separate bedroom where they could lock the door at night and secure bars to the one outside window.

In light of all the tension in our household, it is rather amazing that my parents were married for 52 years before my father passed away from cirrhosis of the liver at the age of 72. They were living in a trailer in Salt Lake City, Utah when he died.

My mother then remarried a retired doctor, who had a home in Oakland, California. He took good care of her. After he passed away, he left her the home. Two of my older sisters came to live with her and, before long she lost the home and everything else. When I last saw her, she was living in a one-bedroom apartment in Fresno, California. Over Christmas 1987, she went to visit my younger sister, Sheila, in Reno, Nevada. While visiting her, she contracted pneumonia and died at the age of 83.

Clearly, my parents had a turbulent marriage. My father's drinking, and subsequent beatings of my mother, was definitely the major source of their problems. Nevertheless, there were times when they displayed signs of affection for each other. I remember when we would all climb into my dad's big truck to travel from Springville to Salt Lake City to take merchandise to my dad's company. My mom would always be seated right by his side, with her hand placed on his leg. I could see the genuine love that she felt for him.

My older sisters were Dee (born in 1925), Ann (born in 1926), Alta (born in 1932), and Viola (born in 1935).

My two oldest sisters were adults when I was a child. My sister, Ann, looked just like the actress Ava Gardner. She was beautiful. I would watch her as she got ready to go out on dates during the war. She would take her eyebrow pencil and draw a line down the back of her legs. You couldn't get nylons during the war, so that's how they did it. I loved watching her getting ready for her dates.

All of my sisters were married by the time they were 16 years old. They were also very wild. They had children early and were married three or four times each. It seemed like they were always with another man or looking for another man. Coming home and dropping their kids off with our mother and then going off again to find another husband seemed to be the norm. They had a built-in babysitter. At least, that's how I saw it.

I was ashamed of them for the kind of lives they led. They were well-known in the area for their rowdy behavior during their adolescence. As a result, the Madsen name had less than a sterling reputation. In fact, many people were surprised I took my maiden name back in the 1980s after my second husband died.

My older brother, Marion, (or "Lucky" as we called him) was born in 1929. He also got married when he was 16 years old.

Before my father married my mother, he was a proud member of the Hole-in-the-Wall Gang, which ran wild in southern Utah. The Hole-in-the-Wall Gang was a group of outlaws. They copied the original Hole-in-the-Wall Gang that ran in Wyoming. They would rob banks and stagecoaches. Being the youngest member of the gang, my father's job was to hold all the horses while the rest of them robbed the bank. My father was in his late teens at the time. He was 20 when he married my mother, who was two years younger.

I often wondered how my mother and father were married in the temple. My mother must have been very religious.

My father was a big man, about 6'5" tall, with a very large frame. My mother, on the other hand, was just 4'11" tall. So they were quite a pair standing side by side. I never considered my father to be handsome, but, my mother was pretty and always kept herself very well groomed.

My father loved telling stories about the Hole-in-the-Wall Gang and their adventures. I remember sitting on my father's knee when he told stories of what they did. He was very proud of their accomplishments. He made good money during their crime spree. And, they were never arrested. Needless to say, we were all fascinated to hear his stories.

After I got married, my parents lived in Salt Lake City. When I visited them, my father would set my young daughter on his knee and share these incredible stories about the Hole-in-the-Wall Gang. She loved hearing grandpa's stories and remembers them to this day.

All but one of my grandparents had passed away by the time I was born, or shortly thereafter.

The only grandparent I knew was my Grandma Madsen, who lived in Salt Lake City. Grandma was large, just like my father. She stood 6'0" tall and, next to her, I felt like a midget. She drove a black 1949 Ford Model T with side fenders.

Grandma Madsen in 1949

Sometimes, when my mother wasn't able to go along for the ride, I accompanied my father on his drives to Salt Lake City for business. On those trips, my father and I would always stop and visit Grandma. But, I could never tell my mother what we did. For some reason, she and Grandma didn't like each other. I never found out why.

I loved my visits with Grandma Madsen. She always had

a pantry full of goodies. She also had some beautiful dolls that she would let me handle, but only if I was very careful. I loved those dolls, and for more than 50 years, I have collected dolls on my own and amassed an impressive collection.

In recent years, I have given one of my collection to each of my granddaughters and great-granddaughters.

While I was in one of my foster homes, I went to spend a week with my grandma. She drove me in her Ford Model T to the state capitol and to the grounds of the Salt Lake City Temple. She explained to me everything about the temple and what they did inside. She told me that someday I would be able to have what they call a "recommend" and be able to go into the temple and do some of the work and maybe even be married in the temple. Temple recommends are given to members of the church who have completed the preliminary steps of faith, repentance, baptism, and confirmation.

During that visit, Grandma bought me my first Book of Mormon, on the condition that I promised to go home and read the whole thing and let her know when I had finished. I fulfilled that promise.

As an adult, I have fond memories of visiting Grandma before my first marriage and after my daughter, Debbie, was born. In fact, Grandma crocheted a pink dress for Debbie.

Every Saturday morning, my mother would drive Pete and me from Springville to Provo, six miles away, for our piano and accordion lessons. I still play the piano today for my own entertainment. My mother could play any instrument she picked up. She played the piano by ear, as well as the violin. In junior high school, I played the violin and the cello.

After our lessons, Pete and I would return home to do our chores, both inside and out. Once we had completed them, we would saddle up our horses and ride into town to see the matinee movie. It was great fun. We would fasten our horses up to a hitching post in the alley and leave them unattended while we watched the movie. Nobody ever bothered them.

At the movies, we would watch the serial and learn the answers to such burning questions as: Where did they leave Mary Jane? Was she left tied up on the tracks with the train coming?

For a nickel, we could go to the movies. For another nickel, we could get two candy bars. What a deal!

No one worried about where we were or feared for our safety. Besides, Pete and I were pretty tough little kids.

Riding horses was one of the great passions of my childhood. When my father became a rodeo producer, I started doing trick riding in his rodeos. I was paid for each performance. It wasn't a lot of money – maybe five or ten dollars – but it was decent money back then.

School wasn't exactly smooth sailing for me.

One of my first recollections goes back to kindergarten. A little boy in the class was giving me trouble, so I removed the hat from his head and tossed it in a tub of water where we were floating paper boats. "Don't mess with Dixie" was the message I sent to him and the rest of my classmates.

The next year, I attended first grade in Orem, Utah. The only thing I remember about that year was the day I asked the teacher if I could go to the bathroom. She said no. So I promptly peed my pants and the teacher sent me home. That was OK because I really didn't like school.

One time, I skipped school for an entire week! My mother made me wear boys' boots to school because I was always taking the heel off of my saddle oxfords for a hopscotch taw (an oversized marker made of rubber). This didn't bother me too much because we would have to pass by a pond on the walk to school. So, I would pack my lunch in my paper sack and just stop at the pond and play all day until that week was over. It was much more fun being at the pond, building a raft, and catching frogs than it was to be in school anyway. After the week was up, I could return to school wearing my regular shoes again.

In case it wasn't obvious, I didn't care much for school. It seemed like a total waste of time to me. I was forever gazing out the window of the classroom, searching for something better to do. Frankly, the only activities I really enjoyed in grade school were recess and lunchtime.

CHAPTER 3

Brotherly love

My little brother, Pete, was born on January 23, 1939, a little less than two years after me. Pete and I were great friends. We were inseparable growing up. We loved to play together and trouble always seemed to find us. We fought so much that as we got a little older, our dad would make us put on boxing gloves and duke it out until one of us got hurt. On most occasions, that was Pete.

One time, I knocked Pete down and he slammed into the leg of the front room dining table, suffering a deep gash over his left eye. He had that scar until the day he died.

Another time, I knocked him through the glass on my mother's bookcase. I was surprised I didn't kill him. After that

Dixie and Pete
(ages 3 and 1)
in St. George

encounter, we both received beatings for breaking the glass in the bookcase. Double punishment, I guess. Especially for Pete.

When we were in grade school, I took Pete down to the slaughterhouse that we had on our property at the farm. I had stolen a pack of my father's cigars from the jockey box in his truck and persuaded my little brother to smoke them. I wasn't going to smoke them until I saw what they did to Pete.

He turned green and began throwing up. I told him that if he tattled on me, I would beat him up. I was one tough sister, but he loved me anyway.

While we were in grade school, we would take out our horses and ride in the culvert along Highway 91. I was aboard my trick riding horse and Pete wanted to ride along behind me. I had a saddle on the horse that day and Pete was hanging on. As I increased the speed and we began to gallop, I saw ahead the neighbors' calf, attached to a chain, feeding in the culvert.

When the calf saw us coming, he jumped in front of us extending the chain straight across our path. I leaped off the horse, but my little brother stayed on. The horse fell on Pete's leg and broke it. Boy, did I get a beating for that one. The more Pete screamed, the more Momma beat me for not watching out for my little brother.

During the winter, Pete and I often missed the school bus. This was by design, of course. We loved to get off the highway, trudge over to the old road, and stand by the stop sign. When a vehicle came to a stop, we would discreetly sneak up behind the car or truck, grab onto the back fender, and slide on the snow and ice all the way to school without the driver knowing we were back there. This practice, known as skitching, certainly added a little adventure to our day and made our journey to school that much more fun.

Pete and I stayed as far away from the house as possible when we were not in school. We would cut large limbs from a big tree in our yard and take large nails from my father's shed. We would secure the nails to the point of our sticks and then take off and head for the swamp about a half mile from our house. We would take our newly-created weapons and see how many toads and frogs we could stab.

On the way down to the swamp, we placed Indian tobacco onto sheets from the Sears catalog from our outhouse – we couldn't afford toilet paper – then rolled cigarettes and smoked them.

Tragically, Pete died of lung cancer. He blamed me to his dying day and said that I was the cause of his smoking. I think he smoked for most of his 66 years.

I often think back to the day Pete died. That day, I lost my longest-standing and dearest friend. We could always talk with each other. We also knew what each had endured – growing up in a family that we wished we had never been born into.

Conversely, I wasn't really close with my older sisters. Truth be told, I really detested them. They were always forcing me to do things I thought were wrong. Then, I'd get blamed when things went awry. And, you know what that meant – Mommy would bring out the belt again.

I don't remember my fourth sister, Viola, being around very much until junior high school. Then, I remember her being sick a lot. Mom would say Viola was too sick to do the chores.

It was only later in my life that I learned my mother and father had given her to a couple who couldn't have children. She lived with them until she was 12 or 13.

That's why I never remembered playing with her, even though she was just two years older than me. Thank God for Pete.

As we were raised during the tail end of World War II, we didn't grow up with a lot of material things. Times were tough and food was very scarce.

I remember eating cans of meat and kidney beans that my mother would get from the bargain basement in Provo.

We were only allowed two pairs of shoes a year and those were obtained through a stamp program of some kind. My clothes were mostly hand-me-downs from my older sisters.

But, we were the first family in our area to get a TV and I remember our neighbors would come over some nights to watch it. So we must not have been that poor.

Considering our large family, one would have thought the holidays would have been a huge burden financially. However, I remember getting almost everything I wanted for Christmas.

Perhaps it was because Christmas was a very special day at our house. My mother and father were married on Christmas day, 1922. They were married in the Mormon temple and we belonged to the Church of Jesus Christ of Latter-day Saints (L.D.S.).

As a child growing up and going to church, I didn't know that Mormons didn't smoke, didn't drink alcohol, and didn't swear.

Christmas also meant it was time for the dreaded fruitcake. Mommy would make this big three-layer fruitcake, containing lots of liquor, a couple of months before December. She would cover it with lots of white icing and then put it way up high on a shelf in one of the bedrooms. She would warn us kids not to touch it until Christmas day.

When the big day arrived, the frosting was so hard you'd break your teeth trying to bite into it. Not surprisingly, I've never acquired a taste for fruitcake.

Fending for myself and experiencing new adventures became second nature for me as a child. I enjoyed the freedom of discovering, exploring, and learning in the great outdoors. This is a passion that has continued all my life. During my formative years, it allowed me to spend a great deal of time away from home, which was my salvation considering the environment in which I grew up.

One of my favorite pastimes was venturing out and lying on top of the haystack. I'd lay there for hours, watching the clouds. I'd try to determine what figures, shapes, and animals I could see in the clouds.

This was generally where I was when my mother would call me. We had so many kids in our family that we never answered Mom's call unless she hit on our name twice. That was the signal that she wanted us and it was time to come in.

One of my favorite escapes was heading out to the gravel pits and spending hours there. When I went to the gravel pits to play, Momma would always make me snacks of graham crackers with frosting between them. I remember the powdered sugar frosting was always pink.

When we moved to Springville in 1942, I started riding horses and doing lots of chores on the farm before and after school.

I changed schools from Spanish Fork to Springville. Our farm was just in between the school bus routes.

It was during this time that my mother and father started to drive to Provo every Saturday night to watch the boxing matches. At that time, my older siblings were out dating or doing whatever.

My parents would drive Pete and me to the theater in Springville, drop us off, and give us money for candy and popcorn. We would watch the movie until we got tired. Then we would move to the front row of the theater, curl around two seats, and go to sleep.

When the boxing matches in Provo ended, my mother and father would drive back to Springville, walk into the theater, wake us up, and take us home. This became our weekend routine.

There was no concern about anyone kidnapping us or molesting us. It was a different time.

Kids today are tired of hearing older generations lament about walking miles through the snow to school. But, that was the case in my childhood.

As we were situated right in the middle of two zones for school bus pick-up, we would have to walk some distance just to catch the bus up the road. And, if we were late completing our chores, we would have to walk the entire way to school. I used to think it was about five miles, but in reality it was probably closer to a mile and a half. As I became an ultrarunner later in life, I gained a better understanding of distances. Nevertheless, we still had to navigate through the snow in the winter.

When I shared this with my own children later in life, they would interrupt me before I could finish.

"Oh, we know what you're about to say," they would interject. "You had to walk miles in the snow to and from school and we won't even ride our bikes a few blocks to school."

My father and another gentleman bought some horses and bulls in 1949 and began to produce rodeos all over the state of Utah.

I started to train my horses and began performing trick riding at my father's rodeo events. My mother would sew all of my trick riding outfits in beautiful red and white satin.

Meanwhile, my two brothers, Pete and Lucky, took up riding bulls, saddle broncos and bareback horses in the rodeos and became professional rodeo riders in many events throughout their lives. They ultimately advanced to winning their divisions in their adult years.

Trick riding, liberty stand – circa 1949, Santaquin, Utah

I started out training my horse, Tony, to perform grandstand climbing onto boxes and then I'd do a liberty stand while the music (*Third Man Theme*) was playing.

In the middle of one of my performances, Tony got all four feet up on the top box and would not move down for me. It was rather embarrassing when I had to get down from my liberty stand and talk him into backing off of the boxes. All the while, the music was playing and the crowd was cheering.

The next two years, I moved from performing with Tony to doing a stunt with my three white horses. I would stand astraddle with one foot on the back of the outside horses flanking the middle horse. We would then jump three different sections of poles. Then I would drop two horses off and do regular trick riding positions hanging from the back of the horse. I would jump from one side to the other and execute the liberty stand as we circled the arena. One missed turn or step could have caused serious injury.

I used to practice on Highway 91 where there was a good culvert along both sides of the road.

I would take my trick riding horse out there and train while people were driving their cars down the highway. They could see me hanging from the back of my horse upside down and volting (jumping) from side to side. Then I'd do the liberty stand while the horse was galloping at full speed.

It was a little daring, but that's the way I approached life — living dangerously and on the edge.

Frankly, I think it's much better than kids hanging around the house or burying their noses in their mobile devices as their source of entertainment today.

The L.D.S. Church has always had a tremendous influence in my life. When I was young, I attended primary lessons on Wednesdays after school. This was for children five to 12 years old. We would go to church where the teacher would instruct us about the gospel. At eight years old, we were baptized in the church and made a member.

My mother would drop us off at church when we were younger. Then, when I started school, we would head over to church after school. There was also Sunday school for children five to 12 years old. I learned the gospel at a very young age and believed in it very strongly. From the age of 12 to young adulthood, we had advanced gospel teaching. It was through attending these meetings that we were taught to abstain from drinking, smoking, and swearing. And, we were taught to be close to the Lord. Viola was the only other family member who was as active in the church as I was.

By attending my meetings, setting my goals, and believing in the gospel, the church helped me to believe there was something bigger and better waiting for me.

CHAPTER 4

Shuffling from place to place

I did my best to stay away from the house and family as much as possible. I played in the fields, rode horses, and did just about anything to keep my distance from my family.

At age 13, I decided to run away from home. I was tired of the beatings from my mother and was always being blamed for everything by my sisters, particularly Alta.

You might wonder how a 13-year-old girl could possibly run away from home. How did I get the money to do whatever I planned on doing?

Well, my father was a hide and junk buyer for a company in Salt Lake City. And when he was on the road, he would leave his checkbook at home with some of the checks signed, just in case someone came to the farm with a sheep hide or cow hide or junk. We were told to give the customer the lowest price they would accept and write them a check. Then we would receive the excess money when Daddy came home, examined the merchandise, and decided what it was really worth. So we learned how to negotiate at a very young age.

Anyway, I took one of Daddy's signed checks, made it out for a certain amount, and got on the bus pretending to go to school. Instead, I went to Christensen's department store in Springville, cashed the check, and bought an orange sweater. I don't know why, because I don't even like the color orange. I also bought a pair of Levi's, some socks, and shoes. I put my school clothes in a bag and bought a bus ticket for Duchesne, Utah and ended up at my brother Lucky's home 100 miles away.

Well, my parents came to get me and, guess what; they gave me a severe beating. They brought me home, put bars on my bedroom window, and locked me in my room at night.

I was not deterred, or maybe I just didn't know any better. I tried to run away again in the seventh grade, but I didn't know how and where to get enough money so I could hop on a bus to somewhere else. I also didn't know which of my older siblings would protect me and hide me from my parents if I showed up at their door.

But, first things first. I needed to get some money.

It was a cold winter day and I was walking to the main street with my sister, Viola. I saw the Texaco service station on the corner and I decided that was going to be my target.

I instructed Viola to keep an eye on the attendant, who was pumping gas at the time. Meanwhile, I would take the money from the cash register. She got scared and tried to run while the attendant caught me with my hands in the till.

To this day, Viola denies her involvement in this caper. She said it must have been my older sister, Alta, because she "would never do anything like that." But Alta was married and had a child, so I knew it wasn't her. Whatever.

We were turned over to the police and spent the night in jail. The next day, we appeared before the judge.

I addressed the judge in a courtroom in Provo. The judge asked me if I were planning to go home and stay or if I wanted to be placed in a foster home. He was very aware of the home in which I had been raised because my older siblings had made quite a name – and not in a good way – for the Madsen family that lived out on Highway 91.

It didn't take me long to tell the judge the whole story. I told him that if I were placed back in my parent's home, I would just run away again.

"I would like to go to a foster home," I told the judge. "But, I would prefer to go to an L.D.S. home because I love my time at church and learning about Jesus."

I lived in two different foster homes. The first one was at an L.D.S. home in Provo, but the family wasn't very active in the church. So I attended church meetings by myself.

I stayed with Mr. and Mrs. Bill and their daughter, Marilyn, who was a year younger than me. She was the product of the mother's first marriage.

I finished seventh grade and started eighth grade there. By that time, Marilyn had moved up to junior high school with me. The family was very wealthy and Marilyn was a spoiled brat. I had never been around people like that before.

It turned out there was an underlying reason why they had

taken me in. They had hoped that another child would help Marilyn learn to share and become less selfish.

I could not figure out how they intended to do that since Marilyn was wearing Jantzen sweaters to junior high, while I was wearing clothes that were purchased from the welfare store.

In fact, I spent the next summer picking fruit so I was able to buy one Jantzen sweater. That brand was all the rage at the time.

Marilyn didn't like junior high school as none of my friends wanted her around. She was just too "hoity-toity" as my friends called her.

One Saturday morning during eighth grade, the welfare case worker showed up at the door and announced that she had a new home for me. I learned that Marilyn had thrown a fit and wanted me out of the house.

So it was off to another foster home. This one was in Pleasant Grove, about 12 miles north of Provo.

I would be living with an elderly couple named Horace and Elda Gillman. They were very committed to L.D.S.

They had both lost their spouses early in their first marriages and each had six children. Together, they raised a blended family of 12 children.

All of their children were married, in the service, or somewhere outside the home when I arrived. I would get their full, undivided attention.

They had horses and other farm animals. Mr. Gillman was thrilled that I knew how to ride and could do chores. And, we all got along well.

Mrs. Gillman was very strict. I couldn't leave my room in the morning until my bed was completely made and the room was tidied up.

On Sundays, we went to our church meetings. Then we returned home, went to our rooms to rest, then read the scriptures and returned to church at 6:00 p.m. for our last meeting of the day.

I was thriving at the Gillmans and delighted to be there. By this time, I was in the ninth grade in junior high.

I learned to cope with all the turmoil and challenges I faced in my childhood by living in my own world. I occupied my time by watching and observing shapes and figures in the clouds. And, of course, I attended my primary classes at the L.D.S. Church.

I learned about the gospel and it kept me on a straight path. I didn't want to follow the direction the rest of my family had gone. My goal was to get married in the temple and raise a family.

Certainly, it was disappointing to move from one foster home to another, but I wound up with a wonderful family in a loving home. We shared common principles, values, and beliefs. I knew that regardless of what I had endured, my goals had not changed. I could rise above it all. It was this determination that pulled me through.

I always believed there was a better life waiting for me. If I worked and lived the gospel and carried out the things I needed to do, I would achieve my goals.

There weren't any drugs back in those days. And I never considered seeking the help of a psychiatrist or therapist. For one thing, I wouldn't have been able to afford it. I always had someone to talk with – a close friend, a teacher, or the bishop at the church. When I had to move from one home to another, I knew that I could always seek advice from my bishop. He gave me money for a bus ticket to go live with one of my siblings. I always knew from my studies in the church that I was going to meet someone, get married in the temple, have children, and live a beautiful life.

Throughout all this upheaval, my younger brother, Pete, stayed with my parents. Eventually, he moved out of the house at 15 and went to live with my brother, Lucky, in Duchesne. That's where Pete met his wife. He got married at 16. His wife was 18.

At the time, Pete passed for 18. He went to work for the Gilsonite mines in Bonanza, about 100 miles east of Duchesne. Later, he became a contractor and, among other projects, he built enclosures for the San Francisco Zoo and many tunnels.

Both Pete and Lucky were professional rodeo riders and made good money at it. Lucky rode with hall of fame rodeo rider, Casey Tibbs. They were quite successful. Lucky rode saddle bronc and bareback. Pete was a top Brahma bull rider.

My older sister, Alta, discovered I was living with a foster family in Pleasant Grove and came out for a visit. During her visit, she informed me that my parents had moved to Phoenix, Arizona. She told me they were really sorry for the way they had treated me. She implored me to give my parents another chance.

As a result of Alta's persistence and tenacity, I was about to leave a wonderful foster home to move to Phoenix and live with my parents again. That would prove to be a big mistake.

I soon discovered my parents hadn't changed one bit. I was entering tenth grade in Phoenix and had been there less than six weeks when the trouble started.

I was coming home from school one day when a police car pulled up beside me. I was arrested because my mother had called the police and told them I was a prostitute.

My mother later told me she did this to get even with me for what I said about my family in the courtroom in Provo.

I stayed in a detention center until they could give me a physical and get my records transferred from the courts in Provo. My sister, Viola, and her husband, Leonard, arranged to come down to Phoenix from Mesa, Arizona and take me to live with them while I finished high school.

Two days before Viola and Leonard were scheduled to arrive, five girls in the detention center began planning a breakout. I refused to participate. I told them my sister was coming to take me to live in Mesa and I didn't want to be part of this scheme.

So one night they tied me to the bed with sheets. When the night guard – a big woman – arrived, all five of them jumped her. She was stabbed with a knife one of the girls had taken from the kitchen.

The guard was left sprawled on the floor in the shower

entry. As soon as the girls opened the back door, the sirens began to blare.

I have no idea what happened to the escapees. As for me, I was transferred across the driveway to the children's detention center to stay for the next two days.

I was familiar with the children's center as they had been letting me out every day after the first week to help take care of the babies and children that had been removed from their parents' homes. I stayed there until Viola and Leonard came to pick me up and take me to their home.

I remained with Viola, Leonard, and their first child, John, for a little more than a year. We got along well.

However, I wasn't finished bouncing from place to place. My next move was from Mesa to Portland, Oregon to live with my oldest sister, Dee, and her family.

After having been there for less than a week, my brother-in-law, James, tried to put his arms around me while I was at the sink peeling potatoes for dinner.

I turned around and said, "Don't touch me or I will ram this knife right through your fat gut."

He backed off.

But then he proceeded to take my young niece into the bedroom and raped her. I had no idea for how long this disgusting behavior had been going on, but my sister made no attempt to stop it.

I packed up my clothes and went to visit the bishop of the ward in which they were living. I asked him for help getting to Lucky's home in Duchesne. He gave me money and accompanied me to the bus depot to get my ticket to Duchesne.

CHAPTER 5

Nice to meet ya, cowboy

I was 16 years old, going on 17, and had moved from one bad situation to another.

I arrived in Duchesne to live with Lucky, his wife, Betty, and their four kids in a one-bedroom trailer. I slept with three kids on a pull-out couch.

One day, I was in Roosevelt, about 28 miles away, with my sister in-law, Betty. We were sitting in Lucky's pickup truck and I was feeding a bottle to my nephew, Johnny.

We noticed two cowboys walking down the street. They waved to Betty as they approached the truck. I recognized one of the men, but I didn't know the other one. He was the most beautiful man I had ever seen. At this point, I was definitely not paying any attention to feeding my nephew.

The two cowboys sauntered over to my side of the truck. The one I knew was Bill Lewis. I had met him while he was competing in saddle bronc riding in my father's rodeo circuit.

"Hi Dixie," said Bill. "This is a good friend of mine, Willis Akelund."

I just stared at Willis, my mouth wide open.

"Are you going to be at the Neola Rodeo this weekend?" asked Bill.

"Yes, both of my brothers will be competing," I replied.

"Willie and I will be competing as well," said Bill. Willis was known as Willie.

"See you there," I said.

After they left, I told Betty that Willis was the best-looking man I had ever seen. At that moment, I looked down and saw that the milk I was feeding Johnny had spilled all over the truck. No use crying over spilt milk.

That weekend, I attended the Neola Rodeo with my brother, sister-in-law, and family. Sure enough, Willis came over, sat on the fence and talked with me until his bull came up for him to ride.

He asked me some questions about myself and then invited me to go out to dinner with him, along with Bill and his girlfriend. I said yes.

The next day, Willis asked me to ride over to his parents' home in Vernal, Utah, about an hour's drive from Duchesne.

He was in the army and had just returned home from boot camp in Colorado. He was on leave before being shipped out to Korea for 18 months.

We spent parts of the next three days together. We joked around, kissed a bit, and at one point he pulled my bra strap. I spun around and slapped him as hard as I could. He quickly realized this wasn't going anywhere past the kissing.

"Would you marry me after I get home from Korea?" he later asked me. "Would you wait for me?"

I was both stunned and flattered. Here was a man, who I had just met three days ago and who looked just like Elvis Presley, asking me to marry him.

Of course, I said yes. I had nothing else to do.

I waited and wrote to him every day for 18 months. He, in turn, wrote back every day for 18 months.

At this time, I was working as a waitress at a café in Roosevelt. It was time to find a place of my own. All I could afford was a room in a sleazy hotel. My room was at the end of the hall and was sparsely furnished with a cot and a hot plate burner. I shared a bathroom with everyone else in the hotel. It was located at the other end of the hall.

At night when I had to go to the bathroom or shower, I would get my things ready, open my door, lock it, and run as fast as I could to the bathroom and then lock the door behind me. When I was finished, I would repeat the dash to my room at the other end of the hall. Boy, was I scared! I was only 16 at the time, but passed for 18 to get the job at the café.

It wasn't long before I also started working at night as an usher at the theater to earn a little extra money.

One day while waiting tables at the café, the man who worked across the street came in for his morning coffee. He was a manager at the Safeway grocery store and he always talked with me. This day, he asked me if I would be interested in working for Safeway. They would send me out to Salt Lake City for a week of training. When I returned, I could stay in a granny apartment in their basement. I could tend to their two little girls when they wanted to go out, provided I wasn't working my night job. It was a perfect situation for me. I was thrilled to find a better paying job and to get out of that fleabag hotel room.

CHAPTER 6

Family life

Willis returned from Korea and we got married 12 days later on March 11, 1955. Not much of a courtship, unless you count the 18 months we were apart and writing to each other every day. I was 18 years old. We were very much in love and very happy.

When our daughter, Debbie, was born on December 23, 1955, it was a big turning point in my life. I finally had something of my own. I had this beautiful little girl. We worked together, we played together, we did everything together. She was the light of my life.

Then, my son Corey was born on August 30, 1958 and I loved him to death. I didn't think that I could have any more children as I wasn't able to get pregnant for quite some time. Then, four years after Corey was born, I got pregnant with my third child. Our son, Chad, was born on November 14, 1962. We called him "Blessy" because we felt he was a gift from God.

I was still attending church when I met my husband. While Willis was a member of the church, he didn't attend. After Chad was born, he decided he wanted to become active in the church. He wanted me to take him to the temple. That had been my goal in life – to be married in the temple and have my children sealed to me for time and all eternity.

Willis decided he would quit smoking and drinking and became very active in the church. We went to the temple in Manti, Utah and had our children sealed to us.

When you're married in the temple, you are sealed together for time and all eternity. However, Willis's newfound commitment to the church was short-lived.

About a year later, some of his buddies moved back into town. Almost immediately, Willis started smoking and drinking again. At the time, he was working at the Gilsonite mines in Vernal.

When I objected, Willis said, "It doesn't matter because I married you in the temple. Regardless of what I do, you'll never leave me."

We had bought our first home in Vernal. It was a three-bedroom home on 10 acres. We had a wonderful life. We had animals and a garden. Every year, I canned all the fruit and vegetables from our garden. We deer hunted together. We did Little League together.

When I played semi-pro softball in my 20s and early 30s, I would travel to tournaments on the weekends. We played all over the western states. Corey was our batboy. I made him a uniform and he traveled all around with us. We did a lot to-

Vernal Dinahs softball team in 1960. Dixie in front row, third from left

gether. My softball days ended when I went to work as a nurse.

Debbie and I were very close until she turned 13. Then she became rebellious.

That was about the time her father said, "I'm not going to church anymore."

And Debbie followed suit.

"If Daddy doesn't go to church, I'm not going to church, either," she declared.

Then Corey decided he wouldn't attend church, either. Before long, I was going to church by myself.

I soon discovered Willis was a jealous man. He didn't like it when another man looked at me. He would fly into a rage.

Today, couples find out a lot about each other before they get married. They live together before getting married. In our case, I had only known Willis for three days before he left for Korea. Then, when he returned home, we immediately got married.

On January 3, 1963, tragedy struck my family. My brother, Lucky, his wife, Betty, and three of their children burned to death in a fire at their home in Bonanza. I took in the four surviving boys (ages 14, 12, nine, and seven) and raised them. The fifth surviving child, a girl, went to live with another relative. Including my six-week-old son, Chad, I was raising seven children at the age of 26.

This was a very tough time for me. I had just given birth to my third child and I thought I would never have another child.

At the time, Willis had been injured working in the Gilsonite mines. A pipe had dropped on his hand and he was transported to Salt Lake City to have surgery on the first finger of his right hand. A pin was placed in it to try to save the finger.

When we got word of the tragic fire, I asked Willis to drive out to Bonanza and collect the five children who had survived the fire. I needed to stay with our children and take care of them.

He returned with the four boys and one girl, who went straight to the hospital with severely frozen feet. Then she went to live with an aunt.

Meanwhile, the plumbing in our house had frozen up. We lived on the farm with one small bathroom. All the pipes in the house had frozen as the temperature that night dipped well below zero. All this happened on January 3, 1963.

Willis and his friends, Bill and Sheldon, got a blow torch and went under the house to warm up the pipes so we would have some running water and be able to flush the toilet with all the people coming and going.

While they were under the house un-freezing the pipes, the pin in Willis's finger froze. In a few days, gangrene set in and Willis was rushed to Salt Lake City where they had to amputate the first finger on his right hand.

He would be unable to work for a long time.

When my late brother's four boys arrived at our house, they said they wanted to stay with us. And, in a state of shock, I agreed to take them in and didn't think anything of it.

To say life would become pretty hectic for me was an understatement.

I had seven children to take care of and get ready for school. When I reflect on it and think of the turmoil and craziness in our lives at that time, I wonder how I kept my sanity.

A few weeks later, I started bleeding very badly and had to be rushed to the hospital to undergo a hysterectomy. Chad had been such a big baby and I had so many stitches that I guess that was the only thing that could have been done.

Although I had already had three children and, Lord knows, I had my hands full with my brother's four children, the thought that I couldn't have any more children of my own was difficult to accept.

To compound matters, we were having a hard time making ends meet as Willis was out of work for well over a year.

CHAPTER 7

Trying to maintain my sanity

There were times when – after putting all of the kids on the school bus – I would just sit down and cry.

I would say to myself: "What on earth are you doing? You're only 26 years old and trying to raise seven children."

But I couldn't cry for too long because there was too much work to do.

On one of my visits to the doctor with my baby, I told him about my predicament. He sat me down.

"This baby sleeps every day," said the doctor. "When he sleeps, you need to lie down and take a nap. Take the phone off of the hook, don't let anything disturb you. Dixie, if you don't do this, you are going to lose your mind."

I took the doctor's advice and started to take a nap every day when the baby slept. It wasn't much, but it did help.

One night after fixing dinner for the family, I got up from the table after the blessing to get something I had forgotten. When I returned to the table, there wasn't a stitch of food left in any of the bowls. I got up from the table, walked out to the front porch, and sat down and cried my eyes out.

How was I ever going to learn to cook enough food for all of these kids?

As I was sitting there crying uncontrollably, the front gate opened. I raised my head to see the bishop coming up the walk.

I tried to wipe away my tears and look him in the eye, but I started crying again.

"I was sitting down to dinner," he said. "And, all of a sudden, I felt like I should come over and see you. What can we do for you and this family?"

"You can start by teaching me how to cook for seven kids and two adults," I said. "When I first got married, all I knew how to make was tuna fish sandwiches and pea and potato soup."

He laughed.

"You'll be OK," the bishop assured me. "We'll help make sure that you are."

The first time I realized what on earth was I trying to do taking care of all of these kids was when I took all of them into town to buy shoes.

We were walking across the street at the light when I saw my reflection in the window of the JCPenney store.

Here I was with a baby in my arms and three kids on either

side of me walking across the street to the department store to buy shoes for the whole gang.

That image really shocked me. What on earth was I trying to do? How were we going to manage?

When Pete and I played together as kids, I always pretended to be Superwoman and would put up my armor to defend myself. But, what kind of armor would I need to be a mother to seven kids? It was a good thing we had a charge account at the JCPenney and Montgomery Ward stores.

But we were getting into more and more debt. Chad was four years old when I decided to get a job. I left Chad with a lady, who had six children of her own, while I went to work as a secretary for a collections agency.

My routine was quite exhausting. Each day, I would get all of the kids ready for school, go to work, come home to fix dinner, then get the kids' clothes ready for school, and pack their lunches.

I would stay up most of the night, sewing shirts for the boys and dresses for Debbie. And, if lucky, I got a couple hours of sleep.

There was a lot of friction with my late brother's oldest son. He was 14 when he moved into our home. Consequently, he did not stay with us for that long. He was kind of traumatized after watching the fire destroy his family and his home. He would run away and go back down to Bonanza and try to live in the abandoned little houses by himself. We couldn't do anything with him. He would take guns with him. If anyone came near him, he would shoot at them. He lived an isolated existence.

Fortunately, the other three boys got along really well with my kids. Debbie had the most difficulty with them, being the only girl. She had no tolerance for the boys. Lucky's kids were very different from mine. They had to be groomed. They weren't used to having meals at regular times. They would go down into the cellar and get bottles of peaches. We had a large farmhouse and we converted the attic into a boys' dorm. When I went up there to clean, I'd find bottles of half-eaten peaches and half-eaten boxes of cereal. They would just take food and hide it in their living quarters.

Lucky's kids had to adjust to going to school every day – something they weren't used to in my brother's house – and going to church. The youngest one had a few problems in that he had polio when he was little. He had a little bit of a deformity in his legs and walked with a limp. He had been spoiled so badly by my brother and he had become very hard to control in school.

At Christmas and Easter, I would get a good buy on material and would sew a dress for Debbie and matching shirts for all the boys.

The sewing classes I took in high school really paid off. I was able to make a lot of our clothes, including Western shirts for Willis and many outfits for me.

To add to my duties, I served as PTA president at my

daughter's school and taught a Sunday school class at church.

Saturday was laundry day. There were no automatic washers or dryers, just a wringer washer and tub. I would hang clothes on the line to dry. Then there was ironing, cleaning the house, and getting the kids and clothes ready for church on Sunday.

Our only automobile at this time was a pickup truck. It wasn't very practical once we took in my brother's children. Willis would have to take us to and from church in shifts. On Sundays, church started at 8:00 a.m. and ended at 7:00 p.m.

It wasn't long before we got a car.

Then, one day, I bumped into the wife of one of the two doctors in Vernal, a town of 6,000 residents. She was a registered nurse. She asked me if I might be interested in becoming a nurse. Then I could work for them. *Why not,* I thought to myself.

I attended St. Mary's Nursing School for my basic training and then went to work at Dr. Stringham's office as a nurse. I would spend the next 27 years of my life working as a nurse.

I stayed in private practice so I could be with my children on the weekends.

Nursing is definitely a calling. I love taking care of people and I love the compassion that I am able to show people. In addition to being trained as a nurse, I became an x-ray technician.

My passion for nursing probably goes back to my childhood. I always had compassion for my animals and took care of them all of the time. This compassion probably helped me get through the tough times in my life.

The movie *Jeremiah Johnson* was being filmed in Vernal. The star of the movie, Robert Redford, was in town. During the filming, his horse had kicked him and he fell back against a tree, injuring his shoulder. He was brought over to Dr. Stringham's office. When I received the folder, I went into the waiting room and called "Robert Redford" very professionally.

He was gorgeous.

The doctor came into the office and told Mr. Redford that I needed to give him a shoulder x-ray.

Mr. Redford and I entered the very small x-ray room.

Once he sat down, Mr. Redford said to me: "Ma'am, could you help me lie down?"

I could see he was in a lot of pain.

I was in my early 30s at the time and I thought to myself, *Of course, I can help Robert Redford lie down.*

Then, I quickly reminded myself, *Gee, you've got to be professional here.*

So I stepped up on a stool and put my arms around Mr. Redford to help him lie down. Then he took a seat on the x-ray table.

Just when I had my arms around him, our new doctor, who had recently joined our practice, walked into the room.

And, just as quickly, the doctor said, "Oops!" and immediately shut the door and left.

I said to myself, "I'm going to have a word with him when I get out of here."

I took Mr. Redford's x-ray to get developed and put it up on the board. Then I hunted down the other doctor to tell him what I thought of his antic.

"Don't you ever do anything like that to me again," I demanded.

He just laughed because he had been put up to do it.

Take it from me – kids will say and do the darndest things. I have first-hand experience.

When our kids did anything wrong on the farm, Willis would say to them: "You go ahead and head down to the tree at the end of the lot. Then, break off a branch and bring it back to me. That's what you'll be punished with."

One time, Debbie did something that angered her father.

"All right, Debbie, you go down to the field and get a branch from that tree and bring it back," said Willis. "That's how I'm going to discipline you."

So Debbie walked all the way down to the bottom of the field and broke off one of the biggest branches you could ever imagine. She could hardly pull it up through the pasture.

We were howling as she struggled to drag it up toward her father.

When she finally arrived, Willis said, "I think you've already earned your punishment because I can't even pick up this branch to beat you with it."

Our kids began riding horses at approximately three years old.

(left to right): Willis, Dixie (holding baby Chad), Pete, Johnny, Tim, Debbie, and Corey in 1963, just after the Madsen boys moved in

One day, Debbie and Corey were riding their horses around our farm. Debbie loved horseback riding, while Corey couldn't stand it. He was definitely not a cowboy. As they were riding around the pasture, the horse that Corey was aboard started bucking and threw him off.

Corey returned home crying. "I never want to ride again. Don't ever put me on a horse again."

Chad was born four years after Corey. We got a Shetland pony for Chad to ride. It needed to be broken a little bit. I was too big to break it, but Corey was just the right size.

"Corey, you have to ride this horse," said Willis. "It's already broken and it's not going to hurt you. You need to break in this horse, so your little brother will be able to ride it."

The horse could sense that Corey, who was eight at the time, was not comfortable in the saddle. Every time we put Corey on the horse, it would start running and then stop really fast, throwing Corey off. He ended up screaming. Corey had had enough. Horseback riding was not his forte. He was more into traditional sports.

Chad was definitely an independent sort. After taking in my brother's kids, I didn't have the time to be the kind of mother I needed to be for Chad.

One day, I received a call at the doctor's office. It was from the barber shop.

"Dixie, Chad is here," said the barber. "He wants his hair cut in a Mohawk style."

"You're kidding?" I replied.

"No, he's very adamant about having a Mohawk," said the barber.

"Well, if that's what he wants, go ahead and cut it in a Mohawk," I said. "I'll bring the money down to you as soon as I get off work."

"OK," said the barber.

Chad was thrilled with his haircut. He thought it was wonderful. All the other kids were touching his Mohawk for the rest of the week. But then came church on Sunday. He couldn't wear his hat to church. He didn't think his new haircut was such a neat thing after all.

When Chad was in third grade, I received a call from the principal's office. Chad and his friend had decided to ditch school.

They went over to the rhubarb field nearby and accidentally raised their heads while recess was going on. They were caught. I was summoned to the school to take care of the matter.

Another time, I got a call from the dentist's office.

"Dixie, Chad is here," said Dr. Price. "He wants his back tooth pulled. He started having a toothache. He said nothing that I did helped him, so he wants the tooth pulled. What should I do?"

"You get him ready to pull the tooth," I said. "I will call his father who will come down there and bring him home by the time you're set to pull his tooth."

Things started to unravel in my marriage to Willis when he started drinking and smoking again and hanging out at the pool hall. His jealous nature also reared its ugly head. We were at a dance during the holidays. One of the members in the band – a young man – came up to me during a break. He put his hand on my shoulder because his girlfriend had come in to see the doctor that day. Of course, working for one of the two doctors in town, I knew everything about everybody. He asked me why his girlfriend, Linda, had come in to see the doctor.

"Johnny, you know I can't tell you that," I said. "You'll need to ask Linda."

Well, my husband had been drinking and he noticed the man had touched me on the shoulder. He grabbed me, pulled me out to the car, and beat me very severely. It was in the middle of winter. When we arrived home, Willis kicked me out of the car with his boots. I knew he had broken my ribs. My daughter later found me when she came home from a date. She brought me in the house and helped me clean up. The next morning, I called my doctor.

"My son had left the lawnmower on the breezeway and I tripped over it," I said. "And I think I've broken some ribs. If I come to the office to get an x-ray, could you come and check?"

After taking the x-rays, he confirmed I had broken my ribs. And, I had a black eye.

"I don't think you tripped over a lawnmower," said the doctor.

"Well, doctor, that's the way it's going to be," I said.

CHAPTER 8
Moving to Southern California

I f I had any feelings for my husband at the time, they were all gone. I decided that I would raise my children and get them through high school. Then I was going to divorce Willis. I didn't want to stay with him.

We sold our farm and bought a home in town so I could be closer to the kids' schools and closer to my job. Then I moved into an apartment with my three children.

Meanwhile, one of Willis's friends worked for a big construction firm in San Diego. They had grown up together. He came to Vernal for a visit and asked Willis if he'd like to move to San Diego and bring the family. He thought I would come back to him if we started fresh.

Willis talked me into coming back and we moved to San Diego in 1970. My late brother's children stayed behind with other relatives in Utah when we moved to Southern California.

They have not been in touch with me since then. When they lived with me, I had rules they just weren't used to. When they lived with their parents, they did whatever they wanted to do. If they wanted to go to school, they went. If not, it was no big deal. At my home, they went to school every day and church every Sunday. Before they moved in with me, they weren't used to taking baths and doing chores. They ran wild at my brother's place. My brother was on the rodeo circuit and his kids had no discipline.

My kids were still in school at the time of our move. Debbie, a junior in high school, had been dating the same boy since grade school. She had to leave him behind. Corey had just been elected student body president in junior high school for the following year. He had to leave that behind. Chad, who was in the third grade, thought it would be a huge adventure. The same couldn't be said for the older ones.

But they told me if that's what I wanted to do, if I really wanted to go back and try again with Dad, they would go along. Nevertheless, Debbie was very rebellious. She was very much against moving to San Diego. Her plan was to marry her boyfriend, Robbie, and stay in a little town for the rest of her life.

We moved to San Diego. Instead of my husband drinking and smoking with his buddies in Vernal, he was drinking and smoking with the construction workers in San Diego. Sadly, nothing had changed.

When we first moved to San Diego in August 1970, we

stopped at a Texaco service station right by the airport. My husband went to call the guy he was going to work for to find out where the office was located. As he stood in the phone booth calling his boss, I looked out over downtown San Diego. The planes were flying in and out of the city.

I had agreed to move from a town of 6,000 people to one of the largest cities in the U.S. When Willis returned from the phone booth, I was crying.

How was I ever going to know where my children were? What was going to happen to them while I was working in a different part of town? I had always worked within a few blocks of them. They would be able to walk over to see me, ask me questions, and let me know where they were going to be. I was truly frightened.

As it turned out, within six years they had all left San Diego and I had fallen in love with the city, a city in which I would remain for the rest of my life.

I returned to work right away, while Willis spent more time out of work than gainfully employed.

I saw my children for a few minutes in the morning and then at night. The boys played Little League and learned to love San Diego. I would rush from my nursing job directly to the baseball diamond to serve as team mother and scorekeeper, and to do whatever else needed to be done. Among other things, I created the team signs and stitched decals onto the uniforms.

We bought a home in San Carlos, a neighborhood in the eastern part of San Diego, and I went to work as a nurse for a group of surgeons in El Cajon. Corey loved it here. He fell in love with surfing and became a California dude right away.

On the other hand, Debbie hated southern California and still doesn't like it to this day.

I still had a definite plan. I was going to get my kids through high school and then I was going to divorce Willis.

He knew it was my plan, but he never believed I would go through with a divorce because I had married him in the temple. You don't break up a temple marriage.

Willis became more jealous and more abusive toward me. The children thought at that time it was the right thing for me to do. He did not abuse the kids, but he was very strict.

He coached both Corey and Chad in Little League. He loved doing it and, in a sense, he was living vicariously through them.

Corey always showed great promise as a baseball player. He was a terrific pitcher. When he was 14 years old and in ninth grade, he went away on a spring break camping and surfing trip to San Onofre State Beach, about 60 miles north of San Diego.

While he was gone, a professional scout from the Cincinnati Reds baseball organization, dropped by our house to inquire about his baseball talents. Corey's dream was to be a starting pitcher for the St. Louis Cardinals.

I fondly remember serving as Corey's catcher when he practiced his pitching. I caught him right up until he started high school. I used a regular fielder's glove. No catcher's mitt for me.

Corey's sinker ball was a pitch that had baseball scouts drooling. And, trust me, it was a tough pitch to catch. My glove hand would be so swollen and sore at end of a workout. But I never let Corey know how much it hurt.

In the movie, *Field of Dreams*, Kevin Costner's character, Roy, asked his father: "Dad, you wanna play catch?"

In our house, it was: "Mom, you wanna play catch?"

"Sure, son," was my response.

I retired from catching him at the right time.

Willis was very tough on Corey. By the time he was in the seventh grade, Corey had ulcers. He graduated from Patrick Henry High School and earned a baseball scholarship to the University of Utah. Unfortunately, he tore all of the ligaments in his right knee while stealing second base in a pre-season game in Arizona. He had to come home for surgery.

In those days, knee surgery was a long and painful process. After surgery, he was put in a cast for a week, then had another brace put on for several weeks, followed by many weeks of physical therapy. By the time his rehabilitation was over, he chose not to return to college.

After graduating from Patrick Henry High School, Debbie attended Grossmont College in El Cajon for a year before deciding to move back to Vernal.

At the time, I had been on disability. My broken ribs had created a bile buildup. I would get really sick. The doctor told me that I would never work again. The truth was I was having emotional problems. The stress of contemplating divorce after a temple marriage was very troubling and that was the root of the problem.

I had become tired of Willis not working. Our debts were piling up and bill collectors were calling us at all hours of the day. And I was certainly not going to move back to Vernal. I had lived there for many years and had determined it was not the place I wanted to spend the rest of my life.

CHAPTER 9

Time to move on

I couldn't remain with Willis any longer. I moved into an apartment in La Mesa (nine miles east of downtown San Diego) with Chad, who was attending Grossmont High School. Then I filed for divorce. I told my attorney I didn't want any alimony.

"Dixie, you haven't worked for three years," he said. "You have to ask for something."

"I don't want anything from him because he won't give me anything," I replied.

We were very much in debt. We had to have bankruptcy protection. We had lost everything except Willis's truck and his working tools for construction. We split the money from the home we had in San Carlos.

"If you will not ask for at least five dollars, I will not handle this case," said my attorney.

"OK, ask for five dollars," I said.

"You think you're a super woman and you can go out and get a job?" he asked.

"By February 15, I will have a job," I said.

In early January 1976, I filed for divorce, left Willis's belongings in the house, took my things, and moved into an apartment with my youngest son.

After I divorced Willis, one of the first things I did was join the Arthur Murray Dance Studio. Taking dancing lessons was great fun, and it wasn't long before the instructor was having me perform dance routines at their other studios.

What made it even more enjoyable was that Chad was in high school at the time, and I would come home from my dance lessons and teach him and two of his friends the latest dances. It made them the three most popular boys at the high school dances. Chad and I had a great time together.

When we had moved to San Diego in 1970, I went back to school at Mesa College to get an extra x-ray license to go along with my nursing license. I would make more money with that added credential.

We had an answering machine at home at the time. I scanned the *San Diego Union-Tribune* daily newspaper and placed an ad as a nurse and an x-ray technician. I asked interested parties to call me at my home phone number.

By February 15, I went to work for a group of doctors in the Balboa Park area. They specialized in internal medicine and nephrology. Like I promised my attorney, I landed a job by February 15.

Willis tried to get me to come back several times, but I re-fused. He had his job in San Diego, but then he decided he wanted to move back to Vernal. I decided I wasn't going to move back to that little town.

I had virtually no contact with Willis after 1976. He moved back to San Diego from Utah and married a local woman. Then they returned to Vernal and he lived there for the rest of his life. He died in 1996 after suffering a heart attack.

On one of Chad's visits to Utah, Willis talked him into moving back to Vernal with him.

"We can hunt and fish and do all those fun things togeth-er," he promised Chad.

It broke my heart when my son said he wanted to move back to Vernal to be with his dad.

"Please don't do this," I said.

"Momma, it's OK," said Chad. "I'll come and visit you."

I knew better. If Willis took Chad with him back to Utah, he thought I would go with him, too. I think he held out hope that would happen.

"If you move to be with your father, you cannot move back," I told Chad. "You cannot play your father against me and move back and forth. You make your decision."

I regret saying that.

Unfortunately, for the rest of Chad's life – through all

the problems he had – he thought he could never move back in with me.

Chad moved to Vernal. His father didn't go hunting and fishing with him. Instead, he turned him loose in town. Chad dropped out of school and started running with a gang. He began taking drugs. He was arrested and spent about eight years in and out of jail.

When he had to go to prison, I talked to the attorney in Vernal and asked him to place Chad in a prison close to me. They placed him in a correctional facility near Long Beach. Every weekend, I drove up to see him. Chad would later be released from the correctional facility. He came to live with me and my second husband. It wasn't long before he decided to move back to Utah.

CHAPTER 10

More ups and downs

I had been on my own for about three years when I met a gentleman named Chuck Bernard, who had moved into the same apartment complex. He was an optician who had retired from the Navy. We dated each other for about 18 months. At the same time, my husband in Vernal was still trying to get me to come back to him.

"I want to marry you," said Chuck. "I want you to stay here."

There was no chance I was ever going back to Vernal.

Chuck and I were married for a year and a half. He had been married previously and had two children. His ex-wife and kids were living in Michigan.

During my marriage to Chuck, my son, Chad, came back

to see me in San Diego. There was a warrant out for his arrest in Vernal. I talked him into returning to Vernal and trying to straighten it out. I had just recently married Chuck and he didn't want Chad living with us.

I should have never listened to him and should have kept Chad with me. I should have known better and been a better mother to Chad. And I should have told Chuck that he was staying and I was going to help him out. But I didn't.

Chuck and I loved to go dancing. He was a terrific dancer. One night, we were planning to go out dancing with another couple. After playing a round of golf during the day, Chuck came home and suggested we take a nap so that we'd be well-rested for our night out.

We laid down on the bed and I was curled up around him. He had already fallen asleep and I was still awake. All of a sudden, something hit me and knocked me clear over to the other side of the bed. Chuck had suffered a massive heart attack. I picked him up, laid him on the floor, and grabbed the phone to dial 911. Then I started CPR on him.

I could hear the ambulance going back and forth. I guess they couldn't find the apartment complex. Fortunately, the windows and doors were open and I screamed. The landlady heard me and went out to flag down the ambulance and direct them to our apartment.

Because of my nursing background, I knew when I was doing CPR that he was already gone. I knew that he had a heart problem.

Chuck was just 45 years old when he died on December 3, 1982. I took care of his cremation and sent his ashes back to his mother.

Chuck left me with nothing, except for $5,000 worth of bills from Sears and Montgomery Ward that his ex-wife had run up on his charge card.

He left me with a lot of bills and no life insurance. Everything was left to his ex-wife in Michigan.

It was a painful lesson for me. I learned to never enter into a relationship without knowing that if something happened, I would be taken care of.

After Chuck passed away, I made up my mind I would never marry again. I would just go on with my life.

Chuck Bernard & Dixie in 1983

CHAPTER 11

Discovering running

I was working as a nurse and, because of the stress at home and at work, I had put on weight. I was 41 years old and had tried every diet that was out there. I weighed 140 pounds on a 5'4" frame. I thought that was ridiculous. When I was raising my children, I weighed between 105 and 108 pounds.

The doctors at the clinic in Balboa Park suggested I take up running. They even introduced me to a San Diego running guru, Ozzie Gontang. I started attending Ozzie's running clinics and began training with his group.

Meanwhile, I would drive to work every morning from my condo in La Mesa. To avoid traffic, I would arrive early and carry my work uniform. Dressed in my running gear, I would run each morning in Balboa Park with two doctors from the clinic. Sometimes, I would run longer routes by myself.

My friends would say: "Dixie, you're running alone at 5 o'clock in the morning in Balboa Park – are you crazy?"

"There's nobody that's going to bother me," I said. "Anybody who might bother me is either drunk or asleep."

When I was running, I was able to deal with all my issues. It took my mind off the things going on in my life. When you're running, you can solve every problem in the world. Your mind is very active.

Then, Dr. Roland, one of the doctors in the office, said to me: "My wife and I are running a 5K in Balboa Park in a week. Come run the 5K with us?"

"5K is 3.2 miles," I said. "I've just been running for a short time. My longest run has been two miles."

"No problem, you can do it," said Dr. Roland.

So I agreed to join them on the run. As I was lining up for the start of the race, I heard people talking about "Cardiac Hill." I'm thinking that must mean something. It wasn't long into the race until I found out what "Cardiac Hill" was all about. I was coming off where Highway 163 enters the park and there in front of me was a very steep hill. *Ah, must be "Cardiac Hill."* I thought I was going to die. But I made it up the hill.

I ran really well and finished the race.

About two weeks later, Dr. Roland said, "You know, we're running a 10K at Christmas time. It's in Balboa Park and it's called the Festival of Lights event. Why don't you train for it and run with us?"

Never one to back down from a challenge, I said OK.

I increased my miles in training over the next few months

to compete in the 10K in Balboa Park. By that time, my competitive juices had definitely kicked in.

I knew I was going to do really well in running because I had done well in everything else I tried in my life. I've always had a competitive nature. I joined the San Diego Track Club and started running with that group.

It was interesting that during the Balboa Park 10K, whenever I thought nobody was watching and that I could walk for a while, I'd glance over and notice somebody from the office cheering me on. I knew I couldn't stop and had to keep on running.

After I ran my fourth 10K and placed third in my age group, I knew that I had an aptitude for running. Then I placed second in my age division. And, eventually, I reached first in my age group. Soon I had a room full of plaques and awards earned in 5Ks and 10Ks.

I completed my first marathon (26.2 miles) – the San Diego Marathon from Coronado to Jack Murphy Stadium (now SDCCU Stadium) – in late 1982. Then, running my second marathon, the Mission Bay Marathon in early 1983, I finished in a time of 3:28:13, which qualified me for the Boston Marathon. I later learned that Boston is the only marathon in which achieving a qualifying time is required.

At a track club meeting, my girlfriend, Linda, approached me.

"Dixie, I have an extra application for Boston as you've qualified for it," said Linda.

"What's Boston?" I asked.

I was so naïve.

"Dixie, for heaven sakes, Boston is *the* marathon," said Linda. "And, you've qualified. Today is the deadline to apply to enter the race."

I was conflicted. I was still in the process of getting over Chuck's death.

"We already have our plane reservations and we have a place to stay, so come and run Boston with us," said Linda.

How could I refuse?

"OK," I finally said.

I filled out my application, sent it to Boston, and was approved. With my qualifying time, I was off to run in the 1983 Boston Marathon.

CHAPTER 12

A magical marathon

I was on cloud nine. I ran a lot by myself as I found it to be very therapeutic. I had been running my distances before and after work. It had also been raining in San Diego, which was good preparation for Boston. The Boston Marathon is held on the third Monday in April and it is generally a rainy time of year there. Unfortunately, I wound up catching a cold. When I arrived in Boston, I was running a fever.

At the spaghetti dinner the night before the race, a young doctor was sitting at our table. He came over and touched my forehead.

"Where are you girls staying?" he asked.

It turned out it was the same hotel as his.

"As soon as this dinner is over, I'm going to come over and check your temperature," he said. "You are really sick."

So he stopped by after dinner. My temperature was over 100. The marathon was just hours away.

"You shouldn't run," said the doctor, an obstetrician who lived on the east coast.

He listened to my lungs and said I didn't sound good at all.

"I'm running," I said emphatically.

"As soon as the race is over, I've got to fly back home because there is a woman who is due to deliver at any time," he said. "But I'll be waiting for you when you cross the finish line to make sure you're OK."

The Boston Marathon is an absolutely amazing event. Race organizers bus you out to the start of the race in a little town called Hopkinton. There are people lining both sides of the street all the way from Hopkinton to the finish line of the race at Copley Square in downtown Boston. The course meanders through the countryside and into the city. At the finish line, there are cots set up to take care of the exhausted runners.

I was clad in my San Diego Track Club singlet with tights and shorts. It was the first time I had worn tights in a race. It was quite cold, especially when we ran past the lakes with the breeze whipping up.

As I was running along the route, I heard people shouting, "Way to go, Dixie, way to go!"

I thought to myself, *Who is watching this marathon? I'm all the way from San Diego. And how do they know my name?*

I later learned that the day before the race they publish a paper that is distributed in Boston and the surrounding towns. The paper lists all the competitors – their names, numbers, and hometowns. The locals study the paper and memorize the names and numbers. So, all along the way, these people are able to encourage the runners by calling out their names.

In addition, spectators hand out peanut butter sandwiches and other snacks to the runners. They have their benches and chairs assembled along the route. There are aid stations set up for all 26 miles. It is a truly special event in which everyone gets involved. And, knowing how fickle the weather can be, the spectators are prepared for the elements.

As soon as I crossed the finish line in a time of 3:19:14, my doctor friend was there to meet me. I collapsed. Then I was escorted to a tent where they hooked me up to an IV. I was really sick.

When I returned to San Diego, the doctors at my clinic took an x-ray. It turned out I had pneumonia. They gave me some antibiotics and sent me home to rest and recover.

After Boston, which was just my third marathon, I went on to run 76 more marathons before moving into ultramarathons (races greater than 50 miles long).

I had developed quite a routine. I would run in Balboa Park for an hour to an hour and a half before work. Then I would return to the office, shower, wash my hair, and put on my uniform for work.

After work, I would head over to the gym near my house and work out for another two hours. Then it was over to the yogurt shop for a light dinner, then home to bed before starting all over again the next day.

One day, I was talking with Dale Sutton, one of the members of the track club. He was a race walker. He urged me to try longer distances.

"Dixie, Lake Murray is having its 50-mile run and you're an absolute natural," said Dale. "Come run the 50-miler."

I entered the race and broke the women's (50-59 years) course record with a time of 7:53:07.

People often ask me: "Dixie, what do you think about when you're in the middle of a long run?"

"I think about everything in the world, but I think about two feet in front of me," I reply.

To me, it's a time for tranquility. It is time with myself, time in the mountains, and time with God. I can solve every problem in the world when I'm running.

The lure of running for me is to actually see what I could accomplish. I started out running little 5Ks and kept moving up in distance. As I've often said, whatever your mind is committed to do, your body will follow along.

Competing in Santa Ana 10K in 1985 where Dixie won age division 40-50 years

I love the awards I've earned from running. I love placing in my age division. I realize I've been an inspiration to younger runners. When I started running ultramarathons, I was about 20 years older than the other competitors. They looked up to me. They were my support. The camaraderie you feel with the other runners is incredible. We all look out for each other.

I wish I could still run. I still walk three to four miles every day. I still venture down into the canyons near my home for hikes.

I've often wondered how many bears, cougars, deer, coyotes, eagles, and hawks I've encountered on my runs. I fondly remember having to jump over a rattlesnake during the Angeles Crest 100 through the Angeles National Forest just to reach a rock on the other side.

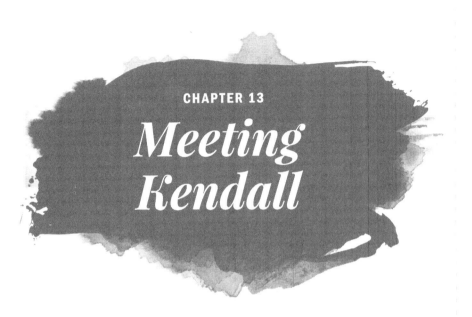

CHAPTER 13

Meeting Kendall

After Chuck had passed away, I wasn't thinking about meeting a man right away. After losing two husbands, I was in no hurry to find a third one.

The San Diego Track Club held get-togethers on the weekend. On Sunday afternoons, we would meet at a member's home. After going for a run, we would convene for a potluck lunch. We would shower and clean up before lunch.

On a particular Sunday in February 1983, we met near Presidio Park. As I was running up the hill toward the house where the potluck lunch would be held, my eyes spotted a man standing on the porch. From a distance, I could tell he was wearing really tight yellow corduroy shorts. And, he was wearing a green polo shirt.

Wow, somebody needs to dress that man, I thought to myself. *Those colors just do not go together at all!*

As I walked toward the front door, the man said hello. I greeted him as well.

Then I went upstairs, showered, and put on my clean clothes. I returned to the party, grabbed a plate of food, and sat down. The man with the mismatched outfit immediately came over and sat down next to me.

I had known there were men in the track club who were interested in asking me out, but they all knew I was a recent widow. So they gave me some space. But, this man – Kendall, was his name – didn't know my situation. He hadn't been at the track club runs or workouts because he had been injured. This was the first time I'd seen him.

We started talking. He told me he was the CIF (California Interscholastic Federation) commissioner for San Diego Section, which covered all high school athletics in San Diego. He was well educated and very nice. We discovered we both went to the gym, lifted weights, and ran. So we had a lot in common.

As I started to leave the party, he asked if he could walk me to my car. Oh, boy, I just didn't want any part of this. There was no way that I was ready to start having anything to do with another man at this time, or maybe ever. I wasn't ready and I really detested the dating scene.

But, he was a nice guy. So I agreed to let him walk me to my car.

I settled into my sports car and started the engine. Then there was a knock on the window.

"Could I have your phone number?" asked Kendall, as I rolled down the window.

"No," I replied.

I don't think Kendall had ever been told "no" in his life.

"I will not put any pressure on you," he said. "This is the first time I've seen you and I just don't want to lose track of you."

I thought to myself, *Oh well, it's got to start sometime.*

So, I gave him my number.

My condominium in La Mesa was about 10 or 15 minutes away. As soon as I walked through the door, the phone began ringing.

"You call this no pressure?" I said, as I picked up the phone.

"I was just wondering," said Kendall. "Since you like to work out at 5 o'clock in the morning, I was wondering if you would like to work out with me at my gym."

I said OK.

Kendall belonged to the 24-Hour Fitness on Balboa Avenue, centrally located in San Diego. We met there at 5:00 a.m. During the 1980s, women dressed in tights and leggings for their workouts. I made sure my hair was perfect, my makeup was perfect, and that I was dressed to kill in my workout clothes.

Kendall asked me out to dinner that night, and we were together for the next 30 years. They turned out to be the best 30 years of my life.

Kendall had come out of a 20-year marriage and I had experienced two "not-so-hot" marriages. So, neither of us was that anxious to get married again when we first met.

Shortly after meeting Kendall

Kendall and I had been together for a year when he took me out to dinner at Tom Ham's Lighthouse for my birthday in February 1984.

As we were enjoying our dinner, he said to me, "What do you think about getting married?"

After a long pause, I said, "What do you think about running a marathon?"

"You know, I'm running a marathon in December," I continued. "I'll train you for the next nine months and if you finish the Honolulu Marathon, I'll marry you."

"Great, we have a deal," said Kendall.

Then Kendall had the waiter bring a doggy bag to me. I didn't understand why since we hadn't left any food on our plates. I opened the box and an engagement ring was inside. It seemed he was pretty certain what my answer would be.

Kendall found out what it was like to run 20 miles on Saturday, followed up by another long run on Sunday. That was

(Left) Kendall and Dixie competing in the Honolulu Marathon in 1997

(Below) Kendall finishing Honolulu Marathon in 1997

the schedule because it was the only time we could get in our long mileage.

When I was married to Chuck, he would go golfing every Sunday with a group of friends while I would go running 20 miles or so, accompanied by men for the most part. Not that many women were running those distances back then.

I would arrive home after Chuck had returned from golfing.

He would greet me skeptically by saying, "I can't believe you have just been running all of this time."

Kendall and I began our weekend running regimen and kept to it.

One day, we went to visit his mother, Helen, in Santa Ana.

"What on earth are you doing to my son?" she asked. "He's getting so skinny."

"Well, Helen," I said. "He's got to run a marathon in December before I'll marry him."

We continued to train and flew to Hawaii to compete in the Honolulu Marathon. Kendall finished the race. As a matter of fact, he finished ahead of me.

When he passed me with about three miles to go, he tapped me on the rear end and said, "I'm doing everything my coach told me. See you at the finish line."

After the race, we flew to Kauai for a week and were married on December 18, 1984.

Originally, we had planned to get married in the Fern Grotto, a fern covered, lava rock grotto located on the Wailua River on the eastern side of Kauai. But after taking a boat up the river to see the venue, we found it was far too commercial for us.

So we went back to our timeshare, a wedding gift from one of my running friends. We waited until the next day and then went hiking up the mountain at the end of the road.

In the tree Dixie climbed to find wedding spot in Kauai in 1984

As we were hiking back, I decided to climb a palm tree. Kendall came back up the trail, searching for me.

"I'm up here," I said. "Right over there is the perfect place for us to get married."

From that tree, I could see the most beautiful place on a cliff overlooking the ocean. I learned later that it was a *heiau*, one of the old Hawaiian worship places where they worshipped and had hula dancing for years.

We returned to town and found a minister to marry us after having a counsel session with him. He referred us to a photographer.

The next day, the minister, his wife, and the photographer hiked up the mountain with us. At sunset, overlooking the ocean and this remarkable vista, we were married.

I had met a man with whom I was truly in love and who loved me just as much. And we had so many interests in common. The years we would spend together were the very best years of my life.

(Above) At the location of our wedding ceremony in 1985

(Left) Our wedding in Kauai, Dec. 18, 1984

CHAPTER 14

A *new* passion – bodybuilding

Kendall had a lot of responsibilities in his role as CIF commissioner at that time. And I was really focused on my running career and was gradually building a name for myself in the running community. When we came home at night or walked to the gym from work, we never talked about our day jobs. It was time for ourselves.

We enjoyed spending our leisure time together – running and working out. We had been working out together for quite some time and I learned that Kendall was a fitness freak. He had been working out every day of his life. His daily routine included spending two hours in the gym before going to work.

"Why don't you start lifting heavier weights with me?" he

asked me one day. "You have the perfect body for a bodybuilder."

I said OK.

So we started working out with heavier weights. We would do a short run in the morning to the gym. Then, after a workout at the gym, we went to work. After work, we returned to the gym for a two-hour workout. Then I would do my long runs on the weekend.

Before long, I was building a pretty nice body.

Kendall told me there was a contest coming up – the North County Bodybuilding Contest in Carlsbad – and that I should enter.

I wasn't so sure.

"Before I do any of this, I want to see a couple of bodybuilding contests," I told him.

This is the approach I take in everything I pursue. If I was going to run a 50-mile race or 100-mile race, I wanted to crew for somebody before I actually ran the race. I wanted to know all the details and all the potential pitfalls before I jumped in feet first.

So we went to observe this contest. I learned that I had to work on a routine set to music. And, I had to fit my poses to the music.

I went back and worked on my routine, picked my music, and entered my first contest – the Pacific Beach Bodybuilding Contest. I took first place in the middleweight division.

Soon I became a member of the Bodybuilding Association. I never placed any lower than second.

"We've got to do something about you," said the master of ceremonies at another event I had just won. "You keep winning first place in the amateur division. We've got to do something about that."

"OK," I said.

"We have a masters contest coming up," he said. "You should enter it."

The event he was referring to was the masters competition at Balboa Park. It was combined with the 1988 Miss San Diego Bodybuilding Contest.

Not only did I win the California Masters competition, but I also won the Miss San Diego Bodybuilding Contest.

What made it more gratifying was that I was competing in my division against girls who were as young as 20 years old.

Posing in the Miss San Diego
Bodybuilding Contest in 1988 at
the age of 51

Holding the Miss San Diego and California
Masters bodybuilding trophies in 1988

In the morning portion of the event, I was the first competitor on stage. During that segment of the event, nobody knows anything about you – your age, your background, nothing at all. But that's also when the judges really do their job and markdown the participants.

The evening competition, on the other hand, is more for sheer entertainment value.

When I walked out for the evening event, the announcer said: "This is Dixie Madsen. She is 51 years old and a grandmother. She has three children."

I went on stage and performed my poses to the Whitney Houston song, *I Wanna Dance with Somebody.*

As I departed the stage and exited behind the curtain, I was greeted by this little, 21-year-old blonde, who was also taking part in the competition.

"You're older than my mother!" she said. "I'm telling my mother."

I was thrilled. To get my body – my 51-year-old body – to that stage where I could compete and win the contest was quite an accomplishment.

I continued to successfully compete in contests for the next few years and was getting ready to compete in the 1992 Pacific Beach Bodybuilding Contest again. While I was hanging out in the warm-up room, I heard several women talking. I couldn't help but notice their deep voices.

I immediately knew. They were on steroids. Being in the medical profession, I knew the classic indicators of steroid use.

That would be my last contest. I was 55 years old at the time. There was nothing more I could legally do to get my body into the shape to compete against women who were using steroids. It wasn't a level playing field and that's when I stopped competing. I continued lifting weights with Kendall every day, but I was finished with competitive bodybuilding.

Nonetheless, I loved the elation I felt when competing in bodybuilding events. I enjoyed being the oldest person in these contests. Most of my peers were in their early 20s and 30s. It gave me great satisfaction to show the younger generations in these contests that I could compete with them and win. And, hopefully, I was an inspiration to them. My motto has always been: do what you love and compete for as long as you can. And, I hope I taught them that you don't have to quit just because you hit 50.

The expression "life begins at 40" really applied to me. I was able to accomplish so much in my nursing profession, in bodybuilding, and in running from that point on.

I spent the last eight years of my nursing career at Alvarado Sports Medicine Clinic in San Diego. I served as a nurse and x-ray technician. The doctors at the clinic were the team physicians for the San Diego Chargers, San Diego State Aztecs, and the USA Olympic men's and women's volleyball teams.

At the Alvarado Sports Medicine Clinic, they still have a large photo of me competing in the 1999 Western States 100 in Squaw Valley hanging in their office. When ultrarunners visit the clinic today, they say, "Wow, you put me in Dixie's room!"

During my time at the clinic, I conducted physicals for the Chargers players at the Town & Country Hotel in Mission Valley.

The clinic director, Dr. Lee Rice, would warn all the players beforehand.

"Don't mess with Dixie," he said.

The players on the Chargers were huge. I often wondered if the tables would hold up under their weight. They were big guys! Football players are generally in good shape but, by far, the player in the best condition was Junior Seau, who would go on to have a long and distinguished Hall of Fame career in the NFL.

Kendall was CIF commissioner when Junior was a star, two-way player (linebacker and tight end) for Oceanside High School in the mid-1980s. Kendall remembered when Junior's family would run on the field during the game to hand Junior money for all the touchdowns for which he was directly responsible.

Kendall would immediately scold them, "You can't give him money on the field. You have to wait until after the game."

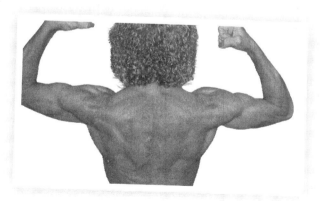

The back of a bodybuilding champion. Dixie won the
Oakland Bodybuilding Contest in 1988

CHAPTER 15

Staggered by more tragedy

The year was 1998. Kendall and I had just pulled into Squaw Valley so that I could get some altitude training completed in advance of the Western States 100-mile race. I had trained well and I figured this year was going to be my personal record for this race, which I had run four times previously.

We had just checked into our timeshare when the phone rang. I picked it up and my daughter, Debbie, was on the line. She informed me that my dear son, Chad, had passed away in Salt Lake City at the age of 35.

My heart was crushed. To be told my beautiful baby boy, whom I had felt so blessed to be able to conceive, had died

(left to right): Corey, Debbie, Dixie, and Chad with
Jackson in front in 1981 in San Luis Obispo

was just staggering. I felt as though my heart had split in half.

I had talked to God so many times during my pregnancy.
I felt truly blessed to be able to have this beautiful child. The
child that I referred to as "Blessy" – because he was a true blessing from God – was gone.

Ever since Chad had been born, I had told various people
that I sensed I was going to get a phone call one day telling me
Chad had died. And on this day, I received that call.

We immediately left our belongings in the condo, returned
to the van, and drove all day and night to Salt Lake City. I cried
the entire trip and talked silently to God wondering how he
could do this to me.

Poor Kendall was beside himself. He didn't know how he
could console me. He had never lost anyone, let alone a child.
How could I comprehend the loss of a child I had watched
grow up? I had such hopes and dreams for him and now they
were extinguished.

When we arrived in Salt Lake City, we went to the apartment Chad shared with his girlfriend. There were a group of people in the apartment. Although Chad had told me he had stopped taking drugs, this group was clearly on drugs. They said Chad had gotten sick, laid down on the couch, and died. They said he had been sick for several days.

Chad and Debbie in 1998 in Casper, Wyoming

The afghan that I had knitted him was gone and they had removed everything he had been lying on. It was pretty apparent to me that he had an overdose, and that his so-called "friends" didn't call for help right away to save him because they, too, were high on drugs.

I don't think a mother ever gets over the loss of a child. It's like a knife that's driven into you. I had lost my baby who I had brought into this world. He was my happy child, an absolute joy to be around. Chad was just six weeks old when I took in four of my late brother's children after the tragic fire. Chad never got the attention he deserved, but he never lost his sunny disposition. He never met a stranger.

Sadly, Chad had let the world get hold of him and drugs ultimately destroyed the child I had loved more than life itself. I've never been the same since that day. Since Chad's death, I've had many conversations with God. For a long time, I had difficulty entering crowds filled with young adults, people about the same age as Chad was when he died.

We made arrangements for Chad to be buried in Salt Lake City. Debbie came from Virginia and Corey arrived from North Carolina. As they tallied up the funeral costs, Kendall's face just got whiter and whiter. We had a nice service for Chad and then drove back to Squaw Valley.

Physically and emotionally, I was in no condition to run the race. But, by the time we returned to Squaw Valley, I had decided to go ahead and run the race and dedicate it to Chad.

Chad's death caused me to return to the church in 2000. It was the only way I could get peace of mind again. As I had gotten married in the temple, our children were sealed to us. I know that I would have him again one day.

When I returned to California to run in the Western States 100 after burying Chad in Utah, I was drained from all the grieving. To compound matters, it had snowed heavily and the first 26 miles of the 100-mile race would be run over six feet of snow. As the snow melted, sinkholes formed periodically over those 26 miles.

It was tough running in snow that deep and, understandably, my mind really wasn't focused on the race like it should have been. At about the 13-mile mark, I noticed a sinkhole about two to three feet wide. The four men running in front of me jumped the sinkhole. When I jumped it, the far side caved in on me.

I could tell immediately that I had injured my left knee,

back, and neck. The guys behind me pulled me back out and I continued to run the race. It was a race I will never forget.

From that point on, I was never the same. From 1998 to 2002, I was running in a lot of pain. I continued with my running career, but needed to have back surgery. After I had healed, I planned my future competitions – in India, Death Valley, and a 50-mile race in Texas. After those events, I had my left knee replaced.

I never had much of a relationship with my younger sister, Sheila. She was just three years old when I went into foster homes. She got married at 16, had four daughters, and lived in Salt Lake City. She started drinking and left her husband and children to go live with another man. I didn't have contact

(left to right): Siblings Sheila, Dixie, and Viola in 1984

with her for many years. Then I heard my mother had gone to visit her in Reno for the Christmas holidays in 1987. During that visit, my mother contracted pneumonia and died. Two weeks later, my sister's husband came home to find that Sheila had shot herself. She was just 41.

It was just another tragic episode in my life. My older sister, Alta, shot herself when she was just 35, the same age as Chad was when he died of an overdose. And, if that isn't eerie enough, my brother, Lucky, was 34 when he died in the house fire. The mid-30s to early 40s were not kind to my family.

I've often thought about my parents after having personally gone through childbearing, adulthood, and the general struggles of life. I wish I could have sat down with my mother for a heart-to-heart chat. As the years have passed, my view of my parents has changed.

My mother had so many children. She had a child – 16 in all – nearly every year for 20 years. Sadly, she lost eight of them. I would have liked to have learned her side of the story. What was going on inside her head? I know I would have had a lot more compassion for her, especially after I had to

With mother (Alta) in 1986
in Fresno

care for seven kids myself and knowing what that all entailed.

I used to think I wasn't anything like my mother. But, as I've matured, I realized I'm more like her than I thought. She used to wax and clean the floors every day. I'm the same way. If I hired anyone to come in to clean, I didn't allow them to clean the floors. I never thought they could do it as well as I could do it. Even though I was only in my parents' home for the first 13 years of my life, I'll never forget how spotless my mother kept the house.

I'm also very meticulous about my appearance. That's the way my mother was. She went to the beauty shop every Friday, right up until the day she died.

If I had a chance to speak with my mother today, I would tell her that I understand. She had to have some way in which to get rid of all that pent-up anger.

For me, I would simply go out for a run to get that release. She used her belt to get that release.

I have come to terms over my relationship with my parents. It was during the war and times were tough. People had lots of kids in those days. They didn't have birth control. Life was very challenging. The war was underway and my parents weren't able to go to the grocery store to get whatever they needed to feed their family.

Pete and I were the only ones who understood what the other was going through. My older siblings were out dating and had nothing to do with us.

Pete harbored a lot of animosity toward my father. My father worked Pete and Lucky really hard. Pete stood only 5'4" tall, but he was very solid. He did physical work as a cement contractor and supervisor. My father was ruthless with his sons.

Pete and Dixie in 1987 in Phoenix

I once witnessed him taking a scoop shovel and hitting Lucky over the head. But, as tough as he was on the boys, he never laid a hand on any of us girls.

Pete and I often talked about how difficult our childhood was. I was with him when he passed away in Phoenix in 2005. When we heard he was in the hospital, Kendall and I jumped into the car and drove to Arizona.

Pete had his arms tied down. His lungs were so bad. He had been on oxygen for years. When I looked at Pete, he motioned to his daughter, Chapita. She brought over a pad of paper and put a pencil in his hand. He wrote, "I love you, sis."

CHAPTER 16

Lure of ultra-distance running

N ever one to back down from a challenge, I turned my attention and energy toward ultra-distance running events after my competitive bodybuilding days ended. I had moved up from 5Ks to 10Ks to marathon distances.

What appealed to me about running – besides the exhilaration I felt when I crossed the finish line – was that there was a time that flashed on the clock that no one could ever take away from me. There were no politics involved in running. When I ran a race, it was my true time. Conversely, the sport of bodybuilding was very subjective. You had to know the judges and, in many respects, it was a popularity contest.

Kendall and I continued training together. He decided he

wanted to compete in the Masters Bodybuilding Contest in Raleigh, North Carolina. We trained and flew out to North Carolina where he finished in second place.

We returned home and became more involved in running. Kendall ran 5Ks and 10Ks. He was a sprinter in college at UCLA and was not into long-distance running. As I got involved in ultrarunning, Kendall followed me and became part of my crew. He followed me all day and night in the car. He handled the supplies that I needed for each race. He was with me every step of the way. Kendall was more excited for my races than I was. He would run a 20-mile segment with me during the ultramarathons.

After I suffered a heart attack in 2010, I had to quit running. Kendall only did one race per year – the Imperial Beach Duathlon. In that event, he would run 1.2 miles, bike 9.3 miles, and then run 3.1 miles.

In 1997, I traveled to Washington State to compete in the Sri Chinmoy 24-Hour Track Race in the hope of breaking some American women's track records.

To achieve this, you have to make sure the track was ratified by the USA Track & Field Association and was also a certified 400-meter track.

I was assured by the race director that was indeed the case before I embarked on the trip.

To set any American records, you must have three people

timing you and one person taking your picture as you hit each of the records – 15K, 20K, 25K, 30K, 50K, 10 miles, 20 miles, two hours, and 12 hours.

The track has to be measured ahead of time with cones placed at each mark. All of this was conducted according to the race director.

I completed the 24-hour race. Everything was in order and the results were sent to the USA Track & Field Association office for ratification.

I returned home feeling extremely tired, but very satisfied with my efforts. However, two weeks later, I was notified that the race director had never gotten the track certified so my records had to be discarded. That was a major disappointment.

Two years later – on November 20, 1999 – I ran the 24-hour race in San Diego with the intention of breaking those records again.

We made sure the track was a certified 400-meter track and was ratified by USA Track & Field Association.

Kendall, along with a friend, Bob Letson, doubled-checked by wheeling the track and setting cones at the exact places I needed to hit.

I arranged for a photographer to take pictures when I hit each record. There were two timers in place to record the time.

Bob had spent a lot of time with the Indians in Copper Canyon, Mexico. Prior to the race, he asked them to prepare a medicine good luck bag (leather pouch) for me. Among the items in the bag was a prayer for my race, along with a hawk feather for my head. I wore it around my neck during the race. Quite often, I wore a bird feather in my cap that I had found on my runs.

On this day in 1999, I managed to eclipse the American records for women 60 to 64 years old for 15K, 10 miles (16.09K), 20K, 25K, 30K, 20 miles (32.18K), and two hours. These records were ratified by the USA Track & Field Association.

A very spiritual and symbolic incident happened at day break as I was coming around to hit my last record. As I was approaching the end of the race, a large hawk flew over my head just as I was rounding the turn. The irony was not lost on me. It was a very beautiful feeling.

What's in a number, you may ask? Well, for me, plenty! I chose the number seven as my lucky number early in my life. I've loved that number ever since. It was Corey's baseball uniform number and that number meant a lot to our family.

When I began running marathons and ultramarathons that was the number I was given at every race. The first race I entered, I asked for number seven. And, every race after that, including the Badwater 135, I was given my lucky number seven.

Award Certificate after having completed the Badwater 135 in July, 2000

When I reflect on my running career, I have a hard time believing some of my accomplishments. They truly astound me.

Over my career, I completed 79 marathons, twenty-seven 50-mile races, two 100K races, twenty-two 100-mile races, one 135-mile race, one 12-hour race, and three 24-hour races.

Looking back, I've had many great achievements, including:

- Competed in the America's Finest City Half Marathon in 1988. Won my age group (50-59) and took home the coveted Mirror Trophy the morning after winning the Miss San Diego Bodybuilding Contest. I had only four hours of sleep!

- Enrolled at San Diego City College in 1989 and ran on the women's cross-country team at the age of 52.

- Competed in the U.S. Nationals Track & Field Championships (Masters) in San Diego in 1989. Entered the discus, long jump, high jump, shotput, and javelin events and won gold medals in all events.

- Competed in the 24-hour race in San Diego, running 90.08

On the San Diego City College cross-country team in 1987 at age 52. Studied health and ran on the track team. Other team members were 20 years old

miles from November 20-21, 1999. I won my age group (60-69).

- Competed in the San Diego one-day, running 81.60 miles from November 18-19, 2000. I had just run a 100-mile race in New Delhi, India three days earlier!
- Broke USA Track & Field records for 50 miles and 100K in 1998.
- Set the 100K record in the 60-64 age group: 11:14:14 at the Ruth Anderson 100K in San Francisco on April 28, 1998.
- Set the 50-mile record in the 60-64 age group: 8:34:19 at the Ruth Anderson 100K in San Francisco on April 28, 1998.
- Broke 15 USA Track & Field records for women in the 50-59 age group in one day! (1997)
- Broke nine USA Track & Field records for women in the 60-64 age group in one day! (1999)
- Voted San Diego/Imperial County Master Athlete of the year in 1998.
- Completed the 135-mile Badwater Ultramarathon in Death Valley in 2000. Was the oldest woman (63 years old) ever to complete the race in a sub 48-hour time (47 hours, 4 minutes).

In June 1989, Kendall came home and announced that the National Masters Track & Field Championships were going to be held in the next few weeks at San Diego State University. Then he proceeded to tell me that he had already signed me up for

Running with Kendall in the 10-mile handicap in Point Loma in 1985

some track events, including the javelin, shotput, and discus.

"This is ridiculous," I said. "It's only three weeks away and we're leaving tomorrow for a two-week vacation to the Bahamas and Aruba."

"That's OK," said Kendall. "You can take your discus and javelin with you on vacation. You'll be able to practice at every place we stay."

"All right, I'll do it," I replied.

So we packed up my javelin and discus for the trip. The javelin is very long and was enclosed in a very suspicious-looking box. I'm sure everybody wondered what was in the box.

After we arrived in the Bahamas, I spent my mornings at the beach throwing my discus and javelin.

When we arrived at the airport for our flight to Aruba, the customs agent asked, "What on earth is in that box?"

"It's my wife's javelin," replied Kendall. "She is going to compete in the Masters Track & Field Championships and she brought her javelin to practice."

He looked at us as if we were from another planet.

"You know, you look like a really nice couple," said the customs agent. "I'm going to double mark this box so you don't have to check it in at any other customs location. With this mark, it'll go all the way through without being inspected again. Trust me, no one is ever going to believe your story."

I continued my training regimen in Aruba by going down to the beach every morning to throw the javelin and the discus.

When we returned home, I checked in for my events at the Masters Track & Field Championships. I discovered that Kendall had also signed me up for the high jump and long jump competitions. I had not competed in the high jump or the long jump since I was in high school. I could have killed Kendall.

When it was time for me to compete in the high jump, I was in a quandary. I couldn't even remember the proper technique. As luck would have it, I was the first competitor up. A woman from Germany was next in line. I pretended to have a problem with my shoe. I asked the judge if I could go second because I need to take care of my shoe. He said that would be fine.

They called up the woman from Germany. As she was performing the high jump, I pretended to tie my shoe. But, in reality, I was watching to see how she approached the high jump. Taking my cue from her, I successfully cleared the jump and ended up winning the gold medal. I also took gold in the long jump, another event I hadn't competed in for many years. And, I took gold in the three throwing events. Five events and five gold medals. I was rather pleased.

Apparently, taking my javelin and discus on vacation paid off after all.

Of the twenty-two 100-mile races I ran, one stands out above the others. Not because it was a triumphant one, but because it taught me more than any other race.

It was an ultramarathon in Old Dominion, Virginia called the Old Dominion 100. For starters, it was organized by the Marines. At our meeting the night before the race, we were told that there would be no water at the aid stations. The Marines didn't think that we needed water to run a 100-mile race. They thought an electrolyte drink would be sufficient. My girlfriend, Toni, who had accompanied me to serve as my crew person, attended the meeting with me.

Kendall had not traveled with me because there was a CIF playoff in San Diego. He told me all along that he could not get away that weekend. It would be the first 100-miler I ran that Kendall was not able to attend.

When they announced the absence of water at the aid stations, Toni and I immediately left the meeting, went over to the nearest 7-Eleven, and bought tons of bottles of water. We placed them in all my drop bags to be delivered to the aid stations that morning. Now I would have an ample supply of water for the race.

As we were walking back to the hotel after purchasing the water, Toni and I noticed a man walking across the parking lot.

"Look at that guy," Toni said. "He almost looks like Kendall."

"He really does look like Kendall," I said.

Then as we moved closer, I said, "It is Kendall. He's wearing my burgundy bicycle shorts."

Kendall had discreetly made arrangements with his assistant at CIF to take over the playoffs and had flown out to Virginia to support me. I was overwhelmed.

The race began and, from the outset, it was a tough race. We traversed through the mountains. And, unlike other races, we weren't allowed to have pacers (someone to run alongside us). Usually, if you were over 50, you were permitted to have a pacer with you at night during 100-mile races. But, as this race was being conducted by the Marines, there were no pacers allowed. I had never been on this course and I was running through the mountains and crossing the Shenandoah River many times. It was very unnerving.

Just before I crossed the river one time, I passed by a campground that was filled with Marines. They were drunk, partying, and whistling at the women running by. I thought it was ridiculous. It was getting dark and they were letting women run without anyone to accompany them. A little while later as I approached one of the crossings of the Shenandoah River, I slipped and fell.

I dropped my flashlight and it started floating down the river. I began crawling by the river trying to retrieve it. Without it, I couldn't continue in the dark. When I finally secured the flashlight, I was soaking wet. And, having crossed the river so many times, I was getting blisters on my feet. I was in agony.

I stopped at the aid station to get my blisters patched up by the Marines. But they didn't do a very good job. When I started running again, the pain returned.

At the next-to-last aid station, I stood on the scale. During

100-mile races, I had a tendency to gain weight. It was because of all the fluids I was taking in. The officials told me if I stepped on the scale at the final aid station and had gained one more pound, they would disqualify me from the race.

Fortunately, I had some special light shorts, a lightweight bra, and super light running race flats in our van. I told Kendall to get the shorts, bra, and racing flats and take them to the last aid station. Then, I went into the woods, stripped off my clothes, changed into my lightweight clothing, and went to the aid station to weigh in. Thankfully, I hadn't gained an ounce. Right in front of the Marines, Kendall handed me my regular shoes and clothing. I put them on and resumed the race.

I was pushing to make the cut off time. I knew I was close. After going through the mountains, the runners head through town to finish the race. They had flares lit to guide us along the way. We had to follow them to navigate the trails. When I hit the edge of town, Toni and Kendall were waiting for me. But there weren't any flares to guide me through the streets to the end of the route. If it hadn't been for Kendall and Toni being there to direct me to the next street and to the fairgrounds, I would have never made it to the finish line in time. I really had to dig deep, considering all the pain I had from the blisters on my feet. And, I knew I was really close to the cut off time. It was a spiritual moment for me. I talked to God for most of that race and I asked Him to help me.

As I crossed the finish line, the announcer declared I had won first place in my age division. It turned out there was a woman in my age group who was ahead of me for most of the race. But she turned down a wrong street, not knowing which way to go. So that's how I took first place in the women's 50+ age group.

This race was important to me because that year I had run enough 100-milers to compete in the challenge of The Last Great Race. That meant that you had to complete six 100-mile races over the summer in various U.S. locations. This was my second race in the series. I had previously run in Vermont and had four races remaining after Virginia. Those races were in Leadville, Colorado; Wasatch, Utah; Squaw Valley, California (the Western States 100); and from Wrightwood to Altadena, California (the Angeles Crest 100).

Unfortunately, I wasn't able to complete all six races. In Leadville, I miscalculated my time when I came over the mountain for the first time. I was cut at the aid station. They simply walk out and cut off your wristband. You're done. It's very humiliating. I would imagine it's a similar feeling one experiences after being dishonorably discharged from the military.

Nevertheless, I went on to finish the last three races in the series, thus completing five of the six races. The next year, I attempted to do all six races again, but ended up getting cut at Leadville 10 miles before the finish. Leadville once again proved to be my undoing.

Dixie competing in Western States 100 in 1991 in Squaw Valley

CHAPTER 17

Family adventures

On a Friday afternoon in July 1987, Kendall came home from work and announced: "I have an interesting trip I think we should take. I've made reservations at our timeshare in Cabo San Lucas. So, tomorrow morning, we're going to get up early and put what we need for a week in our backpacks."

The next morning, we carried our backpacks down to the corner and caught a bus toward downtown. Then we took the trolley down to the border city of San Ysidro. We crossed the U.S./Mexico border and hailed a taxi to the Tijuana International Airport. Kendall had already arranged airplane tickets for us.

Dixie proudly displays the
marlin she caught in Cabo
in 1987

At the beach in Cabo
with Kendall

While we were in the terminal in Tijuana, we bumped into Lance Alworth, retired star wide receiver for the San Diego Chargers and a member of the Pro Football Hall of Fame. He was accompanied by his wife and two children. Kendall knew him.

During our chat, Lance asked, "Where are you headed?"

"We'll be in Cabo," Kendall replied.

"On Monday morning, come out to the docks and we'll take you marlin fishing on my yacht," said Lance.

So, on Monday morning, we went to the docks to go fishing with Lance and his crew. We had been out on the water for a little while when all of a sudden, I caught something on my pole. Immediately, three of his crew grabbed me and led me to the front of the yacht. They strapped me into the captain's seat and instructed me to start reeling.

I was really glad I had been doing bodybuilding at that

time. I reeled and reeled and reeled. It was exhausting work. It seemed like I was reeling for over half an hour.

Then, one of the guys shouted, "Let him go, let him go, let him go!"

"No, no, I can't let him go," I cried. "I've been at this for half an hour."

"No, he's going to break the line," said the guy. "Let him go."

I learned quickly that when you catch a marlin like that, all you can do is release the pole. Then you'll hear, "zing, zing, zing" as the marlin is running. You let them run until they get really tired. Then the crew tells you to start reeling again.

So, I started reeling again and again. I ended up pulling in this huge marlin. I don't recall the actual weight of the marlin, but I do know that when we stood it up, it was twice my height. Once they took the picture for posterity, I gave away the marlin to a group of townspeople to filet it and eat it.

On the north shore of Kauai, there is a beach called Ke'e Beach. A hiking trail extends from Ke'e Beach up into the mountains. The trail ends at a waterfall. Beyond that is the Kalalau Trail.

More often than not, people return from a trip to Kauai and proclaim they've hiked the Kalalau Trail. Truth be told, they've only done a three-mile hike up to the falls. They assumed that was the extent of the hike.

However, the Kalalau Trail goes clear around the opposite

side of Kauai. It's on the Na Pali Coast side. And, the only way you can reach it is by backpacking.

In 2001, Kendall and I planned on tackling this hike. We were equipped with full backpacks for the 11-mile hike. We figured we would be more than ready for the challenge. After all, we've both run marathons (and ultramarathons, in my case), so how difficult could an 11-mile hike be for two fit long-distance runners?

We had our backpacks ready and started to hike the trail at 11:00 a.m. We figured we would be done before dark. We hiked past the falls and proceeded down the trail. It was slippery with lots of red mud. We only took enough food to hike in and hike out. It was getting dark and we weren't anywhere near the end of the trail.

Then we saw a young couple off to the side who were pitching their tent. There was a very small area in which to set up a tent. We had no choice but to stop there and set up our tent. Then it started to rain.

Crossing the stream at the Kalalau Trail in Kauai in 2004

When it came to pitching a tent, Kendall was no help at all. He was an extremely educated man, but being "handy" wasn't his strong suit. If you gave him a hammer, you'd better watch out. He might have killed himself or someone nearby. Fortunately, I knew how to handle most everything. I could put together cabinets and just about anything else.

However, it wasn't easy trying to pitch a tent in the dark.

I kept encouraging Kendall, "You can do this, you can do this."

"*You* should know how to do this," he replied.

Our struggle was apparent to the young couple, who quickly came to our aid and pitched the tent for us. We crawled inside and snuggled into our sleeping bags. However, we didn't bring enough water with us and we suffered from leg cramps all night long. And we had no food left. The next morning, we pulled up our tent and headed back down the trail. It was rough.

In 2002, we planned to do this trip again. This time, we took Kendall's daughter, Kimberleigh, and my granddaughter, Amanda, from North Carolina. The four of us did the whole Kalalau Trail. We started at daybreak (5:00 a.m.) and didn't arrive at the campsite until dark. It took us a full 13 hours to cover the 11 miles of the trail. It was raining and the mud was very slippery.

Twice, Kendall almost went off the side of the mountain. Kimberleigh, who was behind him, grabbed him and pulled him back onto the trail. By the time we reached the last river to cross, Kendall advised us to pitch our tents and then proceed across the next day.

When we were carrying our full backpacks and traversing some of the points on the island, the trail was only one foot wide in many places. We had to hang onto the mountain to navigate this treacherous trail.

Later, we saw a bush woman who lived near the end of the trail. Although she appeared much older than us, she deftly crossed the river. My granddaughter and I looked at each other and decided if the bush woman could negotiate it, we could cross the river and put up our tent on the other side.

Then, Kimberleigh and I put down our backpacks.

"There's no way we're going back down the trail," I said.

We approached the bush people after hearing one of them say he had a rubber boat. We asked him if we could hire him to take us back in two days when we wanted to return. He said he'd be happy to do that. We came back from a hike and examined his boat.

When I returned to our campsite, I said to Kendall, "I'm not getting into that boat. Not with four people with full backpacks and a guide in the boat. I can't swim and I didn't bring my lifejacket."

That night, a really big storm came in. The water got exceedingly rough. We decided it would be a big gamble for us. We asked the bush man if we could leave all of our equipment with him until the water calmed down. We had thousands of dollars' worth of equipment in those four backpacks.

Then I asked if we could hire him to bring our equipment back to the place we were staying in Princeville. He agreed to take our backpacks. Of course, we had no idea if we would ever see our equipment again. We didn't know this man. But we had no choice. We would have to hike out on our own.

The next day, we hiked out. It was miserable. Without a doubt, this was one of the most harrowing adventures we had ever encountered.

Three days later, we were shocked and relieved to see the bush man arrive at our door with all our equipment.

Kendall and I really enjoyed spending time with the grandkids. One of our most memorable family trips took place in 2002 when we decided to take all the grandkids to Disney World in Florida. We had a timeshare there. We used to own three timeshares and we exchanged them for a timeshare close to Disney World. My children, their spouses, all our grandchildren, and one great-grandchild joined us on this trip. Everyone got along really well.

On New York vacation with Kendall in 2005

I was scheduled to have back surgery because of the injury I sustained at the Western States race a few years earlier. Consequently, I was able to get a wheelchair, along with a prescription from my doctor. The kids thought that was great because we could move to the front of the line because their grandmother was in a wheelchair. For some of the rides, I got out of my wheelchair to join the kids.

This was one of many trips we shared with our children

and grandchildren. We would meet at various locations including the Bahamas, Aruba, Virginia Beach, and Cabo San Lucas to enjoy some special family time together.

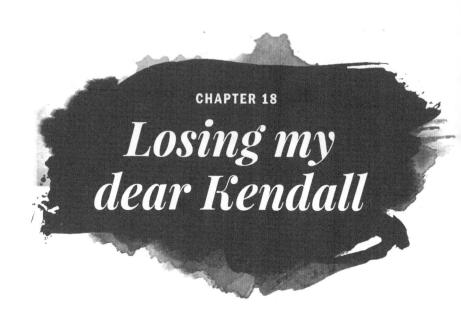

CHAPTER 18

Losing my dear Kendall

Kendall and I had a magical 30 years together. We bought our home in Tierrasanta and watched it rise from the ground up. We had a very happy marriage. All of our kids got along. The entire family got together on holidays. We were a complete and content family unit.

Who on earth would have thought they would meet the love of their life when they were in their mid-40s? Kendall was 50 at the time. We went on to have three decades of complete bliss.

Kendall was my soul mate from the day we meet on a Sunday afternoon in February 1983 at a track club potluck. We were together every day until August 26, 2012.

On that day, Kendall was competing in his favorite event –

Kendall crossing the finish line, just steps before he suffered fatal heart attack

the annual Surf Town Duathlon (running and cycling events) in Imperial Beach. Tragically, he died just moments after winning his age division.

As he crossed the finish line of this race that he truly loved, he collapsed and died four feet in front of me.

He tried to grab a nearby fence, but he didn't have the strength. I just knew he was in trouble. He fell backward and hit his head. But that wasn't what caused his death. The doctor said he had suffered an enormous heart attack.

Ironically, just days earlier, Kendall had celebrated his 80th birthday by hiking up a 10,000-foot mountain near Yosemite with his daughter, Kimberleigh.

God took his spirit in the twinkle of an eye. He finished a

In front of our house in 2009

Celebrating Dixie's 70th birthday party in San Juan
Capistrano in 2007. (left to right): back row: Kimberleigh,
Dixie, Kendall, Loren; front row: Elise, Jolie

race that he loved and also finished his life. I know he would
have wanted to go doing something he loved without suffering
in the process.

I am sure he was struggling and in pain during the race,
but he probably didn't believe that anything serious was wrong.
Other than perhaps not being as prepared as he generally was
for this race every year.

Kendall was such a beautiful man. He had a great phy-
sique, but I guess there was a lot of bad going on inside of that
beautiful body that we didn't know about.

If he had any pain or health issues, he didn't share them
with me. I had been very sick at the time and had suffered two
heart attacks in recent years.

He was very worried about me, so if he had any warnings
signs about his own health, he never shared them with me. He

had complained about the arthritis in his hands and feet and had seen a specialist just two weeks before.

I had been ill, so I never went back with him to get the results of his tests. But several weeks after he passed away, I called and asked for a copy of his test results to be sent to me. When I received them, I noticed his doctor had wanted to put him on medication for his arthritis. But Kendall didn't want to be put on anything at that time, the report said. Also, the doctor had found a heart murmur and had recommended that Kendall see a cardiologist as soon as possible.

But Kendall had declined as he wanted to wait until after the race to see a doctor.

After reading this report, I was quite upset because I had not made the effort to go with him to get the results from the doctor. And I felt badly because he surely had some symptoms that he refused to tell me about.

On that late August day in 2012, I lost my best friend, my lover, my companion, and the person that I could depend on more than any individual I had ever known.

From the moment Kendall met me and learned the story of my life and my hardships, he made it his mission to protect me and make sure I never suffered again. And, that he did right up until his last breath.

I know he would have been upset to leave me to grieve for him so terribly. But I have. Every place I turn, I miss him. We spent so much time together doing the things we loved to do.

We loved each other from the moment we met and discovered we had so very much in common. We worked out together, we ran together, and we raced together. We ran side by side in many races, from 5Ks to 50-milers.

Of course, I trained him to run a marathon in 1984 and we were married in Kauai after the race. We found a very sacred location on top of a mountain and we returned to that same spot every year for many years after that.

In between all of our work, bodybuilding, and racing, Kendall and I did a lot of traveling. For at least two weeks every year, we planned vacations to different places all over the world. Kendall loved to travel. Once he had retired, he planned one trip after the next. It was always a fun adventure as he would find out everything there was to see in the area we would be visiting. So when we left to come home, I knew I had seen it all.

Kendall was CIF commissioner for all high schools in San Diego County and their sports programs from 1976 to 1996. He loved his job, but after 20 years there he was delighted to retire so he could claim every day was a holiday.

Once he retired, Kendall often joked, "I used to be CIF commissioner. Now, I'm Dixie's husband."

He had lost his identity, but he didn't mind it one bit.

Kendall was fun to be around. I swear he never matured past the age of 30. He always maintained that youthful spirit and energy.

He was a good father to his two children, Kimberleigh and Loren, and loved his two granddaughters, Elise and Jolie, with a passion. Sadly, he never got to see Elise graduate from high school and go on to college. He would have been disappointed that she did not follow in his footsteps (and those of his father) to UCLA. Instead, she went to Cal Poly, San Luis Obispo.

I can't bear life without him. I try so hard to put on a good face most of the time, but in my lonely hours I still want him there every minute by my side.

(left to right): Loren, Kendall, and Kimberleigh at Kendall's
induction into the San Diego Hall of Champions

My happiness and joy vanished the day that he left me. I
think of him every day, all the time, and yearn to see him again
every day of my life.

I know that his spirit is in heaven with our Heavenly Father and Jesus and that my spirit will be able to join him when
my life on earth is over.

When I die, I can be sealed to Kendall for time and all
eternity. He is who I want to spend eternity with. I loved him
so deeply and had no idea he would leave me first.

Kendall would often say we were going to be together for
another 25 years. Then he would say we are going to go together. It was his dream that we would pass together. Ironically, I
had a discussion with him just days before he passed away. I told
him I didn't like it that he had arranged separate flights for us,
using our air miles. I didn't like to fly unless we flew together.

We were getting ready to leave for our annual trip to Kauai to visit our sacred wedding place on the mountain. Maybe it

would have been our last time there as the trek up the mountain was getting more difficult each time. He died just six days before we were to leave for a two-week vacation at our timeshare there.

I ask God every day what I am supposed to do without him. Kendall had just turned 80 years old, but he looked so alive and so much younger than what it said on his birth certificate. And, in his mind, he would have lived to be 100 years old. I thought if anyone could make it to 100, it would have been Kendall.

We had been taking care of Coty Akelund, our grandson from my late son, Chad. He lived in Oregon with his mother, but we were very generous with him and brought him down to San Diego every chance we got. We also took him with us to Hawaii three times, as well as to Canada, Mexico, and to many resorts. He was like our own.

In April 2012, he came to live with us. He was right by my side when Kendall passed away. Coty was so devastated when they told him Kendall was gone. He fell to the floor and sobbed as I had never seen a young man sob be- fore. His grandpa was the only male mentor that he had to pat- tern his life after.

Kendall and Coty in August 2012

CHAPTER 19

My family today

After returning to Vernal, Debbie got married and then moved to Wyoming. She was married to Jack Hendrickson for 22 years. They had one son, Jackson, before they got divorced.

Debbie went back to school in Casper, Wyoming and earned her Registered Nurse (RN) degree. I was very proud of her for that accomplishment. To that point in her life, it was the first thing she had started and taken all the way through without quitting. She had taken piano and dance lessons in her childhood and never saw it through. But this time she showed a real commitment. She traveled to Casper during the week, leaving her son and husband behind, before returning to Worland on the weekend while handling a shift at the local hospital.

Leaving Jackson with Jack all week long was not an easy thing for her to do. But it was the only way she could have earned her nursing degree. I was proud of her strength and determination to follow through on that goal.

Debbie is now settled in Chattanooga, Tennessee where Jackson and his wife, Amanda, and their two daughters, Jocelyn and Cecilia, live. She has a nice little apartment, but is having a hard time making it financially. It was a good move for her, though, as she has the satisfaction of being right there to watch her granddaughters grow up. She will be settled when I die. I won't have to worry what she is going to do and how she is going to afford to live.

In June 2017, I flew out to Tennessee to meet up with Debbie. Then we got in her sport utility vehicle and set off on an odyssey. From Tennessee, we traveled the Mormon Trail backward from Missouri to Vermont, and then to Maine for lobster, and then to New York so Debbie could see the Statue of Liberty.

We were on the road for three weeks and had a great trip. We learned and saw a lot about Joseph Smith, the early pioneers, and the translation of the Book of Mormon.

We really enjoyed this adventure. We loved seeing what we had learned about the Church of Jesus Christ of Latter-day Saints, which we believed and had believed all of our lives.

In addition, it was so spiritually motivating to actually see where Joseph Smith received his calling and witness the places the Saints were forced to leave time after time while he was translating the Golden Plates.

I had run 100-mile races through the Wasatch Mountains in Utah over which the pioneers had moved their wagons and carts after they were forced to leave the east and head across the plains. But I had never understood how they could have moved those wagons and carts over those rugged mountains when it was so difficult to run and climb over those mountains during the races in which I competed.

Now, as I followed the trail in the east before they were driven out of Illinois and other states, I knew the ruggedness that awaited them over the Wasatch Mountains.

Losing lives as they went, they still had the faith to follow their prophet's direction to settle in the Salt Lake Valley. And they would build it into a Zion and a place of safety and prosperity.

My faith also strengthened what I had read and believed all of my life.

With daughter Debbie in 2005 in San Diego

I returned from that trip with Debbie having the knowledge that this was the true church of Jesus Christ of Latter-day Saints and where I wanted to remain for the rest of my life.

I have worked in our temple in San Diego doing work for the living and the dead for many years. The work we do is special for those who have passed on and they have their own right to accept it or not. It is submitted by family members and documents all that they have accomplished on this earth.

With son Corey in Raleigh,
North Carolina in 2016

Corey, Dixie, and Debbie in
Harrisonburg, Virginia in 2010

Corey, meanwhile, returned to San Diego after his baseball career at the University of Utah ended. He got married to Donna and they had a daughter, Amanda, while living in San Diego. Then they moved to Raleigh. Ten years later, they had a son, Noah. They lived separately for 12 of the 30 years they were married.

I enjoyed visiting them in Raleigh to watch Corey coach Noah's baseball team and to get to know Noah better. Noah is going to be a great young man. I think he has his head screwed on pretty solidly.

Corey has since moved back to San Diego, a place he has always loved. I hope he can find some happiness in his life as he definitely deserves it.

In 2017, Corey met a new girlfriend, Cindy, who is very special. I really like her. Corey is now coaching the varsity baseball team at Serra High School in San Diego. He will be a great coach for Serra, provided he has some talent with which to work.

Kendall's two children, Loren and Kimberleigh, have treated me very well since I met them many years ago. Kimberleigh has been like another daughter to me. Loren has treated me with love and respect as well.

My sister, Viola, is still going strong at 83. We are the last two survivors from the 16 children my parents had.

I was always under the impression that I was the ninth of 14 children. But when I started researching our genealogy, I discovered another set of twin boys had died with the Rh factor (blue babies).

It seems strange when I think of all my siblings. I hardly knew any of them. Most of them left a bad taste in my mouth. So much so that I didn't want to get to know them. I didn't see much of my older sisters after moving to San Diego. I received a notice through the family chain when they died. The exceptions, of course, were my little brother, Pete, who passed away in 2005, and my sister, Viola.

Viola and I have become closer as we've grown older because of religion. She has stayed active in the church all of her life. She got married in the temple and had five children. Her husband was injured

Dixie, Pete, and Viola in 2003 in Phoenix

in a train accident in Washington State. He had climbed under the train to retrieve some wheat for his farm animals. He thought it was a loose car, but it was attached to the others. The train started up and severed his spinal cord. He passed away in the 1980s.

I remain close with Viola and all her children.

My grandchildren:

Jackson Hendrickson (Debbie's son) lives in Rossland, Georgia with his wife, Amanda, and two daughters, Jocelyn and Cecilia.

Amanda Akelund (Corey's daughter) lives in Raleigh, North Carolina.

Noah Akelund (Corey's son) now lives with me in San Diego.

Coty Akelund (Chad's son) is married to Brittany and lives in Portland, Oregon with one child, Annalyssia.

(left to right): Jolie, Dixie, and Elise in 2016

Kevin Akelund (Chad's son from his first marriage) is married to Jessica with one child, Jayden, and lives in Spokane, Washington.

Elise Webb (Kendall's granddaughter) is in college at Cal Poly, San Luis Obispo.

Jolie Webb (Kendall's granddaughter) is in high school in Santa Ana, California.

My great-grandchildren:

Haley Hendrickson lives in Casper, Wyoming with her mother, Danielle, and stepfather, Henry Blickenstaff.

Great-granddaughter Haley Elliott in 2017 in Casper, Wyoming

Jayden Weimer (great-grandson) in Spokane, Washington in 2018

Jocelyn Hendrickson (great-granddaughter) in Georgia in 2018

Cecilia Hendrickson (great-granddaughter) in Georgia in 2018

Great-granddaughter Annalyssia Akelund in 2018

Jocelyn Hendrickson lives in Rossland with her father, Jackson, and mother, Amanda.

Cecilia Hendrickson lives in Rossland with her father, Jackson, and mother, Amanda.

Step-great-granddaughter Annalyssia lives with Coty and Brittany in Portland.

Step-great-grandson Jayden lives with Kevin and Jessica in Spokane.

I cherish my children, grandchildren, and great-grandchildren with a fierce love – a love that I never experienced as a child.

(left to right) Corey Akelund with daughter
Amanda and son Noah in 2017

Grandson Jackson
Hendrickson in 2018

As soon as my grandchildren turned five years old, I began to fly them to San Diego for vacations. Over the years, I have taken them to many places that I hope they will remember for the rest of their lives. We have enjoyed many adventures together and I hope I have been a loving grandmother to them all.

The story of Kevin Akelund is a special one. I knew my youngest son, Chad, had been married to a woman named Janice and they had a little boy. I received a few pictures of him as a baby. Chad and Janice got divorced and I never heard from Janice or the baby again. My daughter, Debbie, and I had been looking to find him. But it seemed every lead we chased came up empty.

Grandson Kevin Akelund in
Spokane, Washington in 2018

Then, in 2012, Coty, Chad's second son, received an email from a young man named Kevin Akelund.

"Did you have a father named Chad Akelund?" asked Kevin.

"Yes, I have a father named Chad Akelund," said Coty.

"I'm Kevin Akelund, your half-brother," said Kevin.

We finally found Kevin and learned he was married to a woman named Jessica and had a stepson named Jayden. In the summer of 2014, Kevin and his family came to San Diego and we all met for the first time. He is a great young man. He and Coty got along famously.

In fact, Kevin talked Coty into moving to Vernal to work in the oil fields. They lived there for two years before the oil business suffered a downturn, leaving 8,000 oil workers unemployed.

Kevin and his family moved to Spokane while Coty and his clan moved to Portland.

As of this writing, they are both very happy and doing well.

Kendall, Dixie, and Coty in
Kauai in 1997

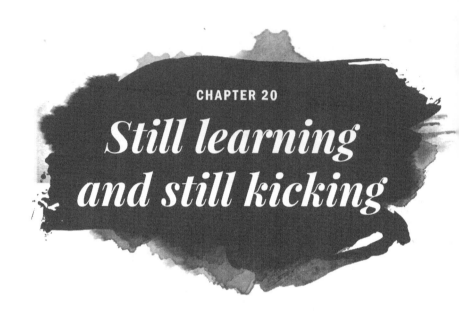

CHAPTER 20

Still learning and still kicking

I have learned so much over the course of my life. Early on, I learned that I couldn't depend on anyone. Unfortunately, on many occasions, people I thought I could depend on let me down. From the age of 13, I learned to depend on myself, set goals, and work toward them.

Often, people I had confided in disappointed me. So I learned to keep my thoughts to myself.

As the saying goes, "once bitten, twice shy."

I would take the fork in the road ahead of me in order to achieve what I wanted to accomplish. Then my journey would proceed in that direction. If, however, it turned out to be the wrong path, I would simply retrace my steps and take the correct road.

I learned that regardless of the storms in my life, eventually the sun would shine again.

When I hear people say, "If I had to live my life over again, I wouldn't change a thing," I immediately smile and shake my head. That's because from as far back as I can remember, I wanted to change my life. I felt there was something better waiting for me if I just worked for it.

So I started on the journey of life. I changed my course whenever necessary to keep working toward what I wanted out of my life.

When you can look in the mirror and learn to really love that person staring back at you, then you have won half the battle. And, if you learn early on to make your own decisions at critical points in your life, then there's no need to look back and blame anyone else for your own mistakes.

I can count on one hand how many times I have taken advice or let someone else's thoughts dictate what I should do in certain situations. And, each time, it was the wrong choice.

Those choices caused me great heartache. In fact, some of those decisions caused severe damage and took years to overcome. Not to mention the pain in mending a fractured relationship with the other person. Nevertheless, I learned to live with that heartache while trying to repair the rift.

No one else is capable of making an important decision for you. Others can only view a situation from their perspective. You see it from the inside and you, alone, should make that decision.

When I die, I am going to be cremated. However, if I were to have a headstone, I would want to have these words etched on it:

"God grant me the serenity to accept the things I cannot change, the courage to change the things I can, and the wisdom to know the difference."

—*Serenity prayer by American theologian Reinhold Niebuhr*

When you make your own decisions, you have no one to blame but yourself. My outlook on life is simple: "Don't look back and don't live in the past. You can't change it."

Just learn to accept the past for what it is, live in the present, and plan for the future. Set goals along the way and then work toward those goals. And, when things get bumpy on that road, dig a little deeper, have confidence in yourself and your ability to climb above the adversity to succeed.

For 30 years of my life, Kendall was the light at the end of my tunnel. He had an uncanny ability to look at everything in a positive manner.

I never heard him make a negative comment about anyone. What a wonderful outlook he had. Wouldn't it be terrific if we could all look at life that way?

I would often ask him, "How do you not worry about certain things? How can you be so happy all of the time?"

"Every day, I have a choice," he said. "And, I choose to be happy."

On Tuesday, December 5, 2017, Corey and I went into the AT&T store to purchase a new phone for me. The person waiting on us had a very bad cold and was constantly coughing. After working with him for two hours, Corey took my phone and cleaned it completely.

Twenty-four hours later, I fell ill. The next day, Corey was very sick.

Corey had to go up to Northern California for a meeting while I was home alone.

At 4:00 a.m. on Sunday, December 10, I drove myself to urgent care in La Jolla where they did a nasal swab. They discovered I had influenza A, which was not covered by that year's flu shot.

They sent me home and told me to rest and drink plenty of fluids. They assured me I would be all right.

Meanwhile, Corey came home from his trip extremely sick and immediately saw his doctor to get some medicine. I made an appointment to see my doctor the next morning.

Corey came into my bedroom and saw me sitting on the side of the bed.

"Mom, I am taking you to urgent care," he said. "You are not going to make it until 7:30 in the morning."

Before we left, I called a member of our church to come and give me a priesthood blessing. I could not hear what was in my blessing. We left and went to urgent care.

By this time, I was going into congestive heart failure. I had suffered a heart attack eight years earlier and had been in and out of congestive heart failure several times. I wore a pacemaker after having suffered a stroke two years earlier in which I had lost the sight in my right eye.

When we arrived at urgent care in La Jolla, they put me on a bed and transferred me to a room.

By then, they had discovered from my diarrhea that I had Mercer pneumonia in the left lower lobe and right upper lobe of my lungs.

I didn't know until three days later that in my blessing from the priesthood of our church I was told I was not going to be leaving. There was still work for me to do.

By this time, I had IVs and antibiotics inserted into my arms. Before long, I went into acute hypoxemic respiratory failure and was asked if I had a DNR (Do Not Resuscitate) order on file. I could not answer. They started oxygen and CPR on me. That was the last thing I remembered.

I was in isolation for seven days as the respiratory therapist hooked me up to a machine every two hours to pound the pneumonia loose and rid it from my body.

Constant antibiotics were being fed to me both orally and through IVs. In isolation, nobody could enter my room without a mask, gloves or gown – not even the doctors.

Over those seven days, I think I had maybe three hours of sleep. That was when the respiratory therapist had to work on a man who was suffering from and eventually died from influenza A in one of the rooms on the isolation ward of the hospital.

I was sent home on December 19. Being a nurse, I was able to give myself my nebulizer treatments every four hours for the next 10 days. More importantly, I was able to sleep in my own bed.

When I returned home, I left a note for my son.

The note said: "When you made the decision to not let me wait and you took me to the urgent care on Tuesday afternoon, you saved your mother's life."

Through God and my priesthood blessing, I have been given more time to live. According to my blessing, there are some things I still need to accomplish.

I don't know whatever they are at this time. But I do know that I will go on, accept those tasks, and complete them as best I can.

I also know that I am looking forward to the day I go home and I am reunited with my beloved Kendall. I believe we will live on for time and all eternity together.

About the
Authors

Born in St. George, Utah, **DIXIE MADSEN** endured and overcame a traumatic childhood filled with heartache and tragedy. Leaving home at age 13 and then living in two foster homes and many temporary situations, Dixie managed to turn her life around after moving to San Diego, California, in 1970. A single parent working as a nurse, she developed a passion for running. Competing in just her

second marathon, she qualified for the famed Boston Marathon and began running in marathons and ultramarathons around the world. Supported by her adoring husband, Dixie became the oldest woman (at 63) to complete the world's most grueling distance race – the Badwater 135 in Death Valley, California – in less than 48 hours. She also earned the Miss San Diego Bodybuilding title at the age of 51. For Dixie, a proud mother, grandmother, and great-grandmother, life certainly began at 40.

A native of Winnipeg, Canada, **SID SHAPIRA** earned his journalism degree from Ryerson University in Toronto. After beginning his career as a reporter, he moved into the area of public relations and corporate communications. Sid's first book was *The Time of My Life*, the autobiography of Jack Leonard, a former Time Inc. executive. Since then, he

has written numerous life stories and family histories through his memoir writing business, Stories Be Told (www. storiesbetold.com). He is also the author of the award-winning nonfiction children's book, *Danny Dog – A rescue dog finds his forever home*. Sid and his wife, Sheryl, live in San Diego, California.